The Yell-Free Parent's Guide to Disciplining an Explosive Child

No-Drama Strategies I Discovered to Discipline My Easily Frustrated Child

Grace Cohen

Contents

Bonus Ebooks (Scan QR Code Below)

Introduction

$\cdot\heartsuit\cdot\heartsuit\cdot\heartsuit\cdot\heartsuit\cdot\heartsuit\cdot$

"Mom, it's almost 8 AM," Thomas said.

I knew this tone already. "Yes, I know honey, I'll be right over there to bring you to school."

"Mom, it's almost 8 AM and I'm gonna be late." Thomas was really persistent.

"Yes, baby. But let me just finish giving your little brother a bath and then I will take you to school." I was feeling pressured at this point.

"Mom, I can't afford to be late! The teacher said I shouldn't be late for class." Thomas repeated.

"Yes, honey. I'm finishing up in a while." This was getting tiring.

"Mom, it's almost 8 AM and the principal is going to ground me for being late." Thomas was relentless.

"I don't know why you say that honey. Don't worry, you are not going to be late. Let me finish this first." I couldn't split my mind between Thomas and my other child.

Thomas' pitch reached a higher notch. "Mom! we've wasted a lot of time!"

"Honey, I told you I'll take you to school after I finish this. Why are you so upset?" My pitch also went up a notch to match his.

"Mom, I want to go to school." Thomas just wouldn't drop it.

"Yes honey, we'll go to school in a while. I still have to attend to your brother. Can you wait quietly in the corner?" I was pleading at this point.

"No, I won't. You keep telling me we shouldn't be late for anything. You said that yourself." The anger was already sketched in his forehead.

"I know you like going to school honey and sure we'll go to school. But your little brother also needs some help." This was becoming a tiring negotiation.

"I don't care. You can give Jack a bath after you take me to school." Thomas was standing his ground.

"Yes, honey..." I was nearing my patience at that point.

"MOM! LET'S GO NOW!!!!" And he steps out of the house, slams the door, kicks the car door repeatedly and sets off the car alarm as neighbors looked on.

· ♥ · ♥ · ♥ · ♥ · ♥ ·

My name is Grace, meet my sons Thomas and Jack, and welcome to our typical weekday morning. This might be an unfair picture of my son, Thomas, because he's not like that all the time. He is actually an adorable kid, participative in school and helpful at times with household chores. But like any other kid, Thomas has his down moments. When he doesn't get his way or if something annoys him, he will make you know he's not happy at all. But unlike the other children I see who just bawl out and cry, Thomas explodes. He can be pretty violent and verbally abusive at times. The worst explosion involved him smashing a couple of windows with his bare hands.

We ended up in the emergency room with a few stitches, a lot of swear words and a bruise in my eye. I just don't know what to do with him anymore. But in his good moments, Thomas is a huggy type of kid, always expressive in his love and affection. But sometimes, I wonder if this is just a prelude to an explosion, the peace before the eruption.

I attend a small support group for parents of 'explosive' children, for my own sanity and also to help me gain some knowledge and understanding about my child's condition. There are around 20 plus parents and we meet every month to share our explosive stories. The sharings are like recounting a horror story happening at home with typically explosive children and their parents fighting the fire either with equal fire or just plain embarrassment. One quite aggressive father shared:

> "I just lost it one day. Adam was just so stubborn. We were supposed to go to my mother's place for Thanksgiving as we usually do every year. But that particular morning, Adam wanted to stay behind and play his online video game. I said he could do it at grandmother's place where there is Wi-Fi. But Adam didn't want to go because he was in the middle of a game that time.

He said he'd consider coming just as soon as the game finished. I came from a couple of days of marathon meetings and sleepless nights at the office only to find my child unwilling to follow a simple command over some games. My mind just went completely berserk. I grabbed his gaming console, threw it out the window and shouted at Adam to get in the 'f*****ing' car. Everybody in the house was shocked at what I did. But I couldn't think straight at that point and we couldn't afford to be late. While driving, I just felt so terrible after that but I had reached a boiling point. Thanksgiving passed by with Adam just glaring at me the whole time. And now, I can't make Adam do anything without myself exploding."

On the one hand, I knew that what that parent did was wrong. It's not a good example to display bursts of anger on your children in such a violent way. But while listening, I couldn't help but feel for the guy. I knew what it was like to be pushed to the edge and I have contemplated such outbursts. But I knew it was never going to solve anything in the long run. Another mother also shared an incident:

"Catelyn is an angel. She is a very sweet and caring daughter, loves to play with her neighbors and makes us letters once in a while. Her favorite color is pink. She likes her dress pink, her shoes pink, her bags and notebooks all pink. And we really made an effort to support her inclinations. But you can't always have pink items all the time. On her birthday for example, we ordered a pink chiffon cake online. We were all excited because the design was really pretty, with Catelyn's favorite unicorns and mermaids all in pink all over the cake. On her birthday, my family came together and we really had a grand celebration for Catelyn. But to our surprise, the cake that arrived was just coated in plain white. The delivery guy explained that there were a lot of orders for pink cakes and there might have been a confusion with the order. When Catelyn saw the white cake, she just blew it. She flew into a tantrum yelling, "I want a pink cake, I want a pink cake" over and over. She smashed the cake with her hands and rolled over the floor. We simply told the delivery guy to return and give us the exact order. It was pretty embarrassing when you couldn't control

your kid in front of everyone. All for a
not-so-pink cake."

While listening to these stories, I felt a little helpless about
our condition. I realized that there are a lot of other parents
who are also experiencing the same difficulties with their
explosive children. We want to be the best parents that we
can, but we just feel so overwhelmed when the explosion
happens. I envy some parents who have it easy with
agreeable children. But I will never trade my Thomas for
any other kid in the world. I just wish there was a way I
could relate with him without exploding myself. And I
worry about what would happen to him in the future if
he continues like this. I am afraid that he might hit other
children in school or that he might be bullied in return.
I worry that when he grows up, he might have difficulties
relating with superiors and bosses at work, in finding and
keeping a stable relationship, in building his own family. I
worry about him constantly and I just feel helpless about
it.

And so this book was written from all those years of
frustration, explosions, tug of wars, kicks and screams, and
quiet moments of tenderness, forgiveness and a genuine
desire to change. I want to reach out to other parents who
are having the same difficulty with their children, who
feel lost and alone. I write this also for our children who

may be very hard to deal with at the moment, but are just yearning to become their best selves given the chance. Lest we forget, these children are our own children and deserve the best parents and chances at life as they can. We owe it to them. I compiled some of my learnings in dealing with an explosive child and I hope I could help you tame the fire. I must declare that I am no medical doctor, nor have I studied extensively on the neurobiological bases of these conditions. But I speak from my heart, from my experiences with Thomas, from my listening to other parents, from my own readings and share with you things that work. I will tell you that it is not easy, nor will you reach a point where you will be perfectly content with the results. This book's goal is not to have very disciplined perfect children who are mostly obedient to you. These are not pets we are training here, but our own independent, willful children. The goal of learning from this book is to equip you with as much knowledge and understanding about your child's condition and how we can make the home a more loving place even with such a condition. Hopefully, this book will help you love them even more.

Chapter 1

The Limits of the Clinic

· ❤ · ❤ · ❤ · ❤ · ❤ ·

The first moment I knew Thomas was rather special was when he was four. Thomas was a very active child, always running up and down the stairs, always tinkering with his toy cars, always curious about what everybody else was doing. And we thought that he was just fine, just your average over-excited kid. One day, I took Thomas shopping with me at the market. I seated him in the back of the car and fastened his seat belt. We were already cruising along the suburbs when I noticed that he kept locking and unlocking his seat belt. I yelled, "Thomas, stop doing that. Please fasten your seatbelt on." And he'd reply, "But mom, is the market too far away? I just want to go out of the car now." Now, the market wasn't really far away, just a ten minute drive from our place. But Thomas was really agitated. He kept squirming at the back, opening and closing the window, knocking his head on the car seat, babbling and singing. We were able to get to the market and as soon as I got him off his seat belts, he quickly got out of the car and started running in circles. I guess he was just excited to go to the market. Maybe he had too much chocolate milk or some of those cookies I baked for him. But I also thought that perhaps there was something else.

Over the next months, I started noticing how Thomas couldn't keep quite still. He was still his usual running up and down in circles self at home. But I noticed that he had difficulty waiting for his turn. One of his favorite words was, "I want it now." When I told him that he will go next month to the theme park he really liked, he just shouted, "I want to go now." When I was trying to fit some clothes in a shopping mall, Thomas already wanted to move to the toy store and shouted, "I want to go now." When his father came home tired from work, Thomas would ask him to play. His father would refuse, but Thomas was adamant and would say, "I want to play now."

We tried everything from bargaining and reasoning with him, to punishing him for rudely interrupting conversations or knocking valuable things at home. We also tried rewarding for a change, giving him incentives like candies or toys when he was able to wait for his turn. All of these worked at some point and all of these failed at some point. I also began noticing that Thomas would keep swinging his legs whenever he was seated for a very long time. I thought it was a nerve disease or something, but the twitching never happened when he was running or actively moving. He was just agitatedly swinging his legs whenever he wasn't doing anything, almost out of impulse.

Other people were already noticing something different from Thomas but we just didn't mind them. My grandmother said I wasn't like that when I was a child and that I should discipline Thomas a little more. I thought that Thomas was just different and that he needed a different kind of parenting from the one I was used to. Thomas was my eldest and I just wanted to be as caring and understanding of him as I can. So I just let the comments slide.

But the day we actually sought help was quite traumatic. It was a typical Saturday morning and Thomas had another episode over his brand new toy train. Apparently, Thomas had chipped the train in multiple edges because he kept crashing it into walls. I was making lunch then when Thomas storms into the kitchen.

"Mommy, my train broke."

"Well honey, that's because you don't take care of them. You should play with your toys a little more carefully." Thomas was quite careless in his things and needed a reminder every now and then.

"Can we buy a new one now?"

"Not now, honey. Your father is away and mom is preparing lunch for us." My mind was starting to wander to the lunch ahead.

"But I want to buy a new train now." As usual, he was indefatigable.

"What did we say about 'now' Thomas? You need to learn to wait. Mommy is busy right now. Plus you have other toys you can play with. You can play with the stuffed bear and dolphins your aunt gave you," I reasoned out.

"But those are lame. I want to buy a new train NOW!" Thomas was starting to shout.

"Don't shout at me Thomas. I don't like shouting in the house." My temper was also rising.

"But you are also shouting whenever you and Dad have a fight. I want to buy NOW!" It was starting to become a screaming contest.

"Honey, that will have to wait." I didn't like where this was going.

"No. I want it now. NOW, NOW, NOW!!!"

And he chucked the toy right at me. Fortunately, it just brushed my shoulders, but it was quite painful. He was fuming and I was quite shocked at what happened. I made him go to his room and grounded him for days. That night, I talked with my husband about the possibility of seeking help. I realized that we couldn't handle Thomas anymore. Maybe we needed professional help. And so, we made a decision to let Thomas be evaluated by a doctor.

Thomas underwent a battery of tests with the doctor. We talked about his behavior and the pediatric psychologist told us to come back every other week. Thomas was diagnosed with Attention-Deficit Hyperactivity Disorder with Oppositional Defiant Behavior. Those were a lot of technical words we had to understand, all of which looked negative and dangerous. We were told that Thomas had to undergo behavioral therapy every week and we abided with that. He was also given some medications when his explosive episodes were uncontrollable and they worked for some time. But I was just worried that some of his medications were causing him to gain weight.

I have a lot of reservations about the whole medical paradigm of managing my child's condition. I associate the doctor or the therapist with handling a life-threatening condition or a contagious disease. I am terrified of doctors, and maybe that fear comes from not understanding what exactly they do. I previously thought that consulting a psychiatrist was only something celebrities would do, or for conditions like depression or anxiety. And I know that this fear is shared by a lot of other parents who are mistrustful or just unfamiliar with the whole medical intervention system. And some parents go far by trying to carry the burden on their own, not seeking medical help until the very end. This chapter was written from my experiences with a lot of mental-health professionals, the valuable work they do and also the limits of their intervention. I think that engaging professional help is the first step in helping yourself and your child.

· ♥ · ♥ · ♥ · ♥ · ♥ ·

Is it necessary to seek help?

Some parents are of the opinion that they can handle their children on their own. This is very much warranted since we grew up not really needing doctors to tell us how to raise our own children. Parents are indeed the primary care givers and know their children best. But we will all reach some boiling point, an instance where we lose control, an episode where we have to admit that we don't know what to do. In these cases, you may want to consider some form of help from people who have devoted their whole lives to understanding your child's condition. You need not suffer alone and bear the frustration and embarrassment of dealing with your explosive child. At that point, you may also need some form of help yourself.

Psychologists and psychiatrists are the usual people you turn to. The primary difference is that the psychiatrist is a medical doctor licensed to give medications. But basically, they both train for long years to study the different mental health issues and how to manage them. There are doctors who are specifically trained to manage children with behavioral problems. There is a special field called Developmental Pediatrics who are tasked with diagnosing and managing children with mental health conditions. Regardless, these professionals will help you understand your situation better. They will be able to advise you on what to do or not to do, but more importantly, how to approach caring for your children.

A note on dealing with medical professionals. Do not be passive clients just obeying your therapists. They will throw a lot of technical words at you like 'Risperidone' or 'autism spectrum disorder,' which can confuse you. It is rather impressive to hear these technical words and you feel as if they really know what they are doing. But when you go home, ask yourself if you really understand what was said and what to do next. If not, then you should demand that the doctor explain the terms in a language that you can understand. In the end, you are going to take care of your own child and not the doctor. If you don't understand what they are saying, then say it aloud, say it promptly. You deserve a good explanation. Be as inquisitive as you can. Ask all the questions you want because these will ultimately help you help your child at home. There will be times when you will feel uncomfortable with some medications or therapies they are proposing. You always have the option to say no, or say no for now. The doctor should help you map out all the possibilities in managing your child as well as the consequences of doing or not doing each intervention. Don't be ashamed that you feel uncomfortable with some decisions because you still have the choice. If you feel that some questions are too offensive or private, then express your reservation. Respect your own process of opening up and engaging in the work of healing your child. Remember that your doctor has the patient's best interests in his or her mind. You also have that. And so, a collaboration between parents and mental healthcare providers must be structured in an open, respectful and trusting environment.

Diagnosing

When your child is evaluated for the first time, they will be asked to complete a couple of tests. Some may involve general IQ tests or your usual pen and paper. Some are observational, wherein the child is made to engage in play and questions will be asked. It may be beyond your scope to understand the different methods doctors use. But in the end, they will give a tentative diagnosis of the condition of your child.

When encountering children who exhibit aggressive, inflexible, and destructive behavior, there are some common diagnoses that may be encountered. I will try to run down on some of these to help you understand. Note that this is not for you to diagnose your own kid. You can Google all you want, but the doctor will still be the most competent person to make that diagnosis. Some of these conditions include:

- Autism Spectrum Disorder

- Attention Deficit Hyperactivity Disorder

- Oppositional Defiant

- Tourette's Syndrome

- Anxiety Disorder

- Obsessive Compulsive Disorder

- Reactive Attachment Disorder

That was quite a mouthful! These terms may be more important to doctors because they studied these conditions longer. But remember that your child's diagnosis does not define your child. Your child's name is still Thomas, or Amanda, or Tracy, not ADHD, Tourette or Asperger. They may fit some of those categories, but they are not in any way reduced to that. The temptation of diagnosis is that it gives you a sense of assurance that you know what your child has and that something can be done about it. But actually, when you read up on all of these diagnoses, the literature is disappointing. Scientists don't actually know what causes these conditions to happen. Sure, there are genetic or environmental causes for some. But the great majority of these conditions don't have a comprehensive explanation like tuberculosis or a heart attack. Having a diagnosis at times may even be counterproductive because you tend to define your child in the terms of each condition. Instead of letting the child behave as they are, you tend to box them in the categories of these diagnoses. So yes, it is good to have a diagnosis just to have some framework to work on. But never let that define your child.

Medications

Again, I repeat that I am not a medical doctor. I do not confess to know how each drug works and the side effects of each. But I think there is value when a layperson tries to explain to other non-medical people how these drugs work. I am not a fan of medications myself because I feel they are unnatural and tinker with the body's natural capacity to heal itself. But when I saw how some of these drugs were able to calm Thomas down, I became more interested in learning about these medications.

Is there a role for medications in managing your child with explosive behavior? We normally associate medications with a disease. If you are feverish, maybe you need an antibiotic. If you have a headache, a pain reliever would do the trick. If your stomach feels gassy, then you can take an antacid to relieve the pain. The body has its own mechanism of healing itself, but medications somehow hasten that process.

Now, can we also apply this to addressing the behavioral concerns of our children? The doctors would all push our children to take as many medicines as they can think of. I hope they are not doing that for profit, but from a sheer genuine desire to help. But I respect medications because the condition of our children is partly physiological. We will explain more about the causes of their condition in the next chapter. But suffice it to say, a strong component of these behaviors has something to do with the imbalance of chemicals and hormones in our body. When a person feels depressed for a very, very long time, certain chemicals are either deficient or in excess which may exacerbate the depression. The goal of these medications then is to supplement what is deficient and to remove what is in excess of the body. Our children are also physical creatures made up of chemicals and hormones. Hence, we cannot deny the fact that some of their behaviors are due to these imbalances. Medications then would be very helpful.

But, as I have praised medications, I will also criticize their unwarranted use. The doctor will be the most competent person to make the decision on which drugs, how strong, how frequent and how long each should be used. But it is ultimately us parents who will be guiding that decision. When we notice that our children are suffering from certain side effects of medication, we should volunteer that information right away. If you feel that your child is not responding well, you deserve a good explanation from your doctor. You can even ask if you can wean off your child from some medications. I am not a fan of just giving medications for the sake of it because it defeats the purpose of health and parenting. Medications are quick solutions to an immediate problem. If you feel down, take an antidepressant. If you feel anxious, take a relaxant. We are simply addressing the symptom and not the real cause of the condition. Hence, medications should only be in aid of the holistic management of our children. When they don't need it, then don't take it.

Therapy

I have never entered a therapist's clinic until I had to attend one for Thomas. I've only seen one from the movies, imagining that the room would have some couch where I would lay down and the doctor would pull out some pendant and start to hypnotize me. I was very wrong. During our first therapy session, the doctor ushered us into a simple room with comfortable chairs. There was no couch and no magic pendant. I was actually surprised when the doctor told me that she will have a separate session first with me and my husband and only then with Thomas together. I kept thinking that Thomas had the problem, not us.

But when the closed-door parent's session ended, I was mildly surprised at how the doctor managed to open up my own issues. She was telling my husband and me that we need the counseling more than Thomas because we are affecting him in some way. The therapy has made me confront my own issues with how I was raised and how I raise my child. It uncovered my own issues with my husband, how I felt alone in raising the children up, how distant he felt from the children. At first, I felt attacked and defensive when I was told that maybe I need to also look at my own issues. But throughout the therapy, I was able to accept that some of my issues were indeed affecting my parenting and my family life. Hence, a great deal of openness is needed when you enter into these sessions. The more you give yourself to the process and not hide anything from the therapist, the easier the healing process can be. Remember that it is not only your child who is undergoing therapy. It is also you benefitting from this process.

I have also tried this phenomenon of therapist-hunting. Thomas' first doctor lasted for about six months before we moved to another. Since then, we consulted five other therapists until we settled with our current one. We were always looking for results, and we wanted it immediately. In the first doctor, we found her style too intrusive. She kept on bringing up our personal issues instead of involving Thomas. My husband had enough of it and told me to look for another. The next therapist was very kind but also did not say a lot. He just kept on repeating the things we said. "So you say that your child is very aggressive?" "Yes," we would say, "but we have been telling you that for an hour." We didn't see how this was going to help Thomas in any way. We kept on looking for a better therapist, one that could deliver results, one that fitted our personalities, one that we could get along with, one that gave brilliant insights, one that charged judiciously, one that looked nice, one whose voice sounded gentle, one that agreed well with Thomas. In short, we were looking for a perfect therapist.

It does not work that way. Our current therapist noticed this behavior of ours and called us out. She noticed that we were shopping for the best therapist and she told us that this was not the best course of action. It was going to be frustrating for us because we had to tell our story all over again, and Thomas would have to warm up once more to a new therapist over and over. Each therapist would have a different perspective and having too many different points of view can confuse rather than clear the problem. She said that we would most likely replace her when she would say something that we don't like or find a fault in her. But this therapist-shopping spree would only cause more damage than solve the problem. If we had a problem with the therapist, it was best that we bring it up in therapy instead of replacing the therapist. She described healing as a momentum, wherein subsequent therapies would lead to better and faster recovery. Hence, when you cut that momentum by frequently changing therapists, then we are also compromising the healing process of our children. It is good to shop around, but it is more advantageous if we stay with a therapist we feel most open to.

Limits

The domain of the therapist is the clinic or the therapy room. Their level of control is only the amount of interaction and conversation that transpires in that room. Beyond that, it is you who will care for your child. You are the one facing the explosions at home. You are the one that will teach your children how to handle their emotions. You are the parent. Hence, the therapist, the medications, the therapy will all just support you in helping your child. They will never replace you, so you can't just send your kid off to therapy and hope they will get better without you. Do not expect that your child will be 100% ok with all these interventions. They will never replace the love and support of us, parents.

Chapter 2

Common Parenting Mistakes

· ♥ · ♥ · ♥ · ♥ · ♥ ·

You've tried everything, I'm sure. If there was a manual compiled on the many ways parents can discipline their kids, you might have read through that and ticked all the boxes. The methods can range from the most understanding and caring of ways to the more physical punishments and screaming contests. These disciplinary methods may fall into the traditional categories of carrot and stick, of rewards and punishment. They may be effective for some or totally useless for some kids. These methods include:What is the main takeaway from this chapter? It is possible to tame explosive children. Do not concentrate too much on feeling guilty about the condition of your child now. Some parents blame themselves constantly because they feel that they are responsible for their child's inflexibility or explosiveness. But there is no point in dwelling in guilt, no good that can come of it. The only way is really to examine ways in which we can understand our child's condition and help them become their best selves. From a self-incriminating mode, we should shift towards actively engaging our children and pushing them to develop themselves further. You will need a lot of help, from your partner to your other children, to the school and the bigger community. And you have me to guide you in this journey towards healing the fire within.

·♥·♥·♥·♥·♥·

The Santa Claus Approach

Of course, the most often used approach is to bribe your kids with all the gifts and toys they want. Follow my command and I will give you the toy truck. Wait your turn and I will give you the cookies. Don't scream and throw things around and I will give you money. This may seem very superficial to some parents who feel that this is tantamount to spoiling their kids. When you give them what they want, you are indulging them instead of teaching your children.

Before you are quick to judge this approach, know that you've done this too often than you admit to. This is the easiest way since positive reinforcement may show an instant result. And yes, this is one of the most effective if used properly. It works because there is a goal that children have to achieve before they are rewarded. Do something good and you will receive something good.

But it loses its potency when you do it more often or when the reward is disproportionate to the task. For example, if you always tell your kids that they will receive a toy when they do their homework, they are going to expect that all the time. When they get the pattern, they will expect more. A simple toy will not cut it. You will have to give more and more, and they won't respond to any other method. This can be rather costly and will also spoil your kids.

Also, if you give them rewards that are not proportional to the task they need to accomplish, they will feel that they will deserve more for more complex tasks. If you give a $1000 video game console for a "B+" paper, then your kids will expect something more expensive when they get a higher grade.

Overall, this method is still effective only if used sparingly and in proportion to the desired task or behavior. As much as you want to lavish your children with gifts just to prevent an explosion, you also have to balance that with disciplining them and making them behave appropriately without the need for positive rewards.

Time-Keeper Approach

Similar to the previous approach, the time-keeper's reward is really about extending time. As parents, we are gate-keepers of our children's happiness. We monitor how much TV they can watch, how many hours they can play with their video game console, or how long they can play outside with friends. You can use the time to your advantage both as a reward and as a punishment. When you tell your kids that if they don't throw a tantrum, they will have an extra hour of watching YouTube, then they will follow.

But this doesn't work particularly when they are already in the process of exploding. You can reason well with a child that is already throwing tantrums by bribing them with more time with consoles. They want it NOW and you will feel helpless to bargain. This only works when children feel a bit calmer and are able to reason out.

The Pleader

When all else fails, the parent would be slumped on the ground, on their knees begging their kids just to stop yelling and kicking. Funny as this scenario may look like, as though a reversal of roles happened, it does occur. It seems embarrassing to ask your kid to cooperate, but sometimes, it is the only thing you can do. The principle here is that you are appealing to their good side. By projecting yourself as weak in reference to their strength, they feel as though they need to cave in to your requests. They might be offset with the change in power dynamics and they might accede to your wishes.

But the glaring truth to this approach is that it just doesn't work. It will only make you less dignified when you plead to your kids. And when you reverse this power dynamic, children will feel that they are more in control of the relationship and will continue to abuse you if given a chance.

The Screaming Contest

The easiest and the most tiring method is, of course, to scream at your kid. If they are shouting at you, the tendency is that you will also be triggered. What ensues is a screaming match that neighbors and everybody around you can hear. Like animals, the one with the louder and longer sound wins the battle. I don't know how long you can hold this match, but it will definitely tire out your kid and yourself. It is not a particularly constructive environment to live in where everybody yells just to get their way.

While this may be effective at first, your child may be desensitized after a while. When you have been used to screaming all day just to get what you want, they will imitate you. If your method works, they will try it out for themselves. By screaming, kicking and throwing a tantrum, they will know how to best get what they want from you. Instead of calming the child down, you are reinforcing more of the anger and the hate when you start lashing out at your children.

The Silent Treatment

When it seems that you can't do anything else, the only solution is just to be silent. This method is actually effective. One, it creates a calm environment where the child will feel awkward when he or she screams aloud. They may have been so used to being shouted at that a silent treatment will alert them that something is new and should be reckoned with. It also taps into their guilt feeling when they are not getting the attention they need.

But it can also work against you if you push it too long. When they are not seeing the results they expect, they can be more agitated and violent. Your increased silence may trigger more aggression in them until you pay them attention. Also, you can't keep silent with your kid for a very long time. They may feel so distant and alone, interpreting your silence as neglect. As with other methods, you have to use this sparingly, or else its potency will be lost.

Grounded Days

The more reasonable approach is really the use of grounding. When children violate preset rules, parents usually disallow certain privileges for a period of time. Because you screamed at Mommy, you don't get to watch TV tonight. Because you kept on nagging about going to the mall when I said we couldn't, then you can't play with your toys this week. Because you pushed your brother because you were angry, you aren't allowed to play outside for a month. This usually works effectively because the privileges are very valued in children.

But when children don't understand the connection between what they did and what the punishment was, then the grounding may not be effective. They will simply interpret it as a temporary setback which they can exact from you after. Because you grounded me for a week, I will be more violent than ever. For some, there is no learning involved, either because the target misbehavior is not specified or the punishment is not proportional to the act. The more effective approach is explaining to them why they were grounded.

You may have your own versions of rewards and punishments. I'm sure you've tried to be creative with all the rewards that you can bribe them and all the punishments you can inflict on them just to get your message across. But sometimes, it just doesn't work. None of it works. They are still as inflexible, as explosive, as impulsive and as relentless as ever. Whether you keep silent or scream, whether you bribe them with toys or threaten them with grounding, they still want to get their own way. And so only two options remain for you: force them to do your way or cave in to their way. Either way, everybody loses.

· ♥ · ♥ · ♥ · ♥ · ♥ ·

Is it me?

At this point, you might start thinking about what caused your child to be as explosive as he is. You try to investigate what are the possible ways that could have led to their behavior. It may not help very much in addressing the problem when your child explodes in front of you. But at least, knowing the cause of their behavior may help you understand the situation better and find ways to help your child.

The literature on many of these developmental problems in children has found out that there is no conclusive cause for these diseases. Yes, you heard it right. Not one specific trigger, gene, parenting style, method of reward and punishment, personality, gender or race can point to the real cause why some children are just more explosive than others. It just happens. Maybe they will know the real cause in the future as they conduct more studies. But for now, the real cause is yet to be found.

Some studies say that explosiveness is genetic. If you have relatives on either side of the family who exhibit the same behavior, then there is a higher chance that the child will also be explosive. But this is not helpful, especially if you can't do something about your child's genes right now. This is just a handle on understanding where this behavior can be traced from.

The child is a product of nature and nurture. So if there is something affecting them in terms of their genes, their environment will also influence their behavior. Children adapt to the personalities of their parents. They look to them for visual cues on how to behave, what to like, which food to taste, which person to avoid, what is scary, what is joyful. Our parents are our models in life and we really look up to them.

Hence, it may be difficult to accept, but our own behaviors may sometimes influence our children. If you have an environment at home where there is constant screaming, physical and verbal abuse, then that will influence your children. Don't be surprised if your child curses if you also curse casually in conversation. Children are very quick to pick up social cues from their parents. They will imitate them because they think that is what is expected.

Of course, it's not always the case. Some families are very gentle and understanding of their children. But they still have explosives in the family. Or living in a violent family does not mean that you will also become violent. Sometimes, you become so averse to that kind of situation that you vow never to have others experience it and you adopt a style that is directly opposite of that environment. And yet, you will still have explosives.

Our parenting styles are also largely influenced by how we ourselves were raised. If your mother is a tiger mom, a strict disciplinarian, forcing you to focus on academics and working hard, then most likely, you are going to apply the same discipline to your own children. If you have quite liberal and independent parents, you may also be as liberal to your children. Of course, there are cases where children hate how they were raised, so they try to raise their own children differently. If you were hit when you were a kid and hated it, you might vow not to hit your own children. But somehow, some of the ways we were raised becomes adopted in our own parenting styles.

We bring these influences and may affect why some kids are more explosive than others. It may be the case that they resent the kind of parenting they are experiencing. But you cannot change your parenting style because that is what worked for you when you were small and you think that will work on your children and on each child. If you force a disciplinarian style on an inflexible child, you are really going to expect explosions every now and then.

Is it them?

Many times, when you feel just so overwhelmed with dousing the fire and confronting your other obligations, you start thinking, "Maybe they are doing it on purpose." You look at your other children and they don't seem as explosive as the other. So the theory that your parenting style may affect your children is not necessarily true because not all of your kids turn out as aggressive. If all of your kids are really explosives, then there is a good cause for a parenting deficiency. But if only one or two in a bunch is more difficult than the others, then perhaps it's not just you but them.

A thought may cross your mind: "Are they just manipulating me?" You try so hard to plead with them to stop whining and follow your command. Yet, they are holding their stand. Can it be that they are just testing your limits, pushing you to the edge and enjoying the ensuing meltdown? Do you think they relish seeing you on your knees pleading that they stop? Is their behavior something they consciously do just to spite you?

The glaring answer to this is really "NO." It is a tempting thought to think that your children have full control of their actions and that this can simply be solved by asking them to change. Remember that they are children first and foremost. Their minds and bodies are still developing. They are still learning how to interact with the world. When they explode, we cannot treat them like adults who have full control of their emotions. In fact, more than getting angry at your inflexible children, you should recognize that they are in need of some form of help. Unlike their peers, something in their brain is unable to cope with the world. Hence, they succumb to this behavior. We will dwell more on that in the next chapter. But we simply have to emphasize that children are not in control of themselves. And given a chance, they will want to be the best versions of themselves. Just like us adults, nobody wants to be the cranky boss, the inflexible partner, the screaming neighbor, or the manipulative friend. We all strive to be good. We exhibit aggressive behavior only when we are pushed to the edge or when we anticipate danger. In the very same way, children only explode because they are triggered. Everybody wants to be their best selves.

Is it impossible?

When you look at the prognosis of the developmental disorders that are commonly diagnosed in explosive children, you would see that most of them are untreatable. They will never be better and the only recourse is just to help them become functional members of society. Therapies are geared towards specific difficulties which will address their functionality. In short, there is no cure, only mitigation of symptoms.

As a parent, hearing that prognosis is quite challenging to accept. You love your children so much, yet doctors are saying that they will never be like other children, that they will remain explosive to the end. It is like facing a lifetime of burdens, having to live and raise a kid who can explode anytime.

But when you think about it, every child isn't perfect. No human is. Others may have the most intelligent or the friendliest kids. But I'm very sure they have their own difficulties too. Ours is just very blatant and obvious. So there is no point in comparing the hand that we are dealt with that of others. The point is that they are our children and we will love them no matter what. A healthy child, a sick child, they are all our children, worthy to be loved.

Though the fact that we cannot change who they are, we can change how they behave and think. The task is not impossible. It is hard, but not impossible. I should know because, after 11 years living with Thomas, I can see a significant change from the time we started therapy and the present. Yes, he still has flares, no doubt about that. But it's not just because I'm used to him that is why I think he is progressing. I can also see that other people are noticing the change in Thomas. He is now more able to wait for his turn. He says, "Please" and "Thank you" when given anything. These might be trivial matters, but for me, these are developments. And you should celebrate each behavior or thinking process that has made them more functional or more agreeable. It is not perfect, but it is definitely some improvement.

The earlier you begin to see the signs of explosiveness and the earlier you seek help, the better the child will be. In the next chapter, we will explore the mind and how it is responsible for all these characteristic behaviors. And the earlier we can intervene, the earlier the brain can develop normatively. It is extremely difficult to handle explosive teens who have not sought help earlier. They are more set in their ways, more independent, vocal, and also more physical. It is not impossible to train them, but it is more difficult than if you had just started earlier.

Chapter 3

The Four Essential Skills

· ♥ · ♥ · ♥ · ♥ · ♥ ·

On our first session with Thomas' first therapist, he brought out this plastic brain model on top of the table. I had never seen a brain before except in pictures, so this was my first encounter with a tangible, albeit plastic brain. It had different colored parts, all with interesting folds and lines all over. Suddenly, a sinking feeling happened inside me as though I knew what would happen next. Is this doctor going to lecture me about Thomas' brain? I wasn't prepared for this. Just looking at that contraption already gave me a headache. I was not prepared to be bombarded with all sorts of scientific jargon and a crash course on anatomy. I wasn't especially good at Science way back in school, and so I was bracing myself for a dizzying lecture.

And then came the prompt. The doctor simply asked: "Would you like to learn about Thomas?"

"Of course!" I said. Who wouldn't want to understand their child? I really wanted to learn everything I could about Thomas. Even his brain.

What he did next really surprised me. "Now, point to any part of the brain and I will tell you what happens when that is stimulated." Interesting proposition. I didn't expect not to be bored with this and the doctor was full of surprises.

So I pointed to the middle top of the brain and the doctor raised his left arm. I proceeded with the left part of that and he raised his right arm. So far, so good.

I pointed to the front part of the brain and the doctor said, "Today is June 15, a Monday." I pointed to another part and he said, "I ate pancakes for breakfast." I pointed to the underside of the brain and he began exhaling and inhaling. I pointed to different parts of the brain and he simply performed a lot of quirky actions and exclamations until I got the point.

"Do you get it? Every part of Thomas' brain and our own brains elicit a reaction in some other part of our body. The more complex the action, the more parts of the brain are involved. Even just a simple movement will trigger different areas in the brain. Are you still with me?"

"Sure." This doctor sure knows my apprehension towards anything scientific. But he got me. I was still glued.

"So the first lesson: there are many different parts of the brain responsible for different actions in the body. Next important lesson: our brains are all developing. When Thomas started out as a combination of his dad's sperm and your egg, his body was starting to develop different parts. As you carry him over in your womb for nine months, his wonderful brain is starting to develop. This wonderful brain connects Thomas to the other parts of the brain. Certain connections called 'nerves' relay information from the outside to Thomas via his brain. Are you still with me?"

"So far, yes." Thomas' brain wasn't exactly in my mind when I was pregnant with him. I just knew he was kicking all over the entire time.

"Now, as Thomas grows up, his brain also becomes more developed. In fact, it is in childhood that most of this development is taking place. When he sees something new, one part of the brain is stimulated and grows. Whatever he sees, smells, hears, tastes, and feels forms one part of his brain. In fact, the brain keeps on developing until the age of 25. And yet even now, the brain keeps on developing the more we read, remember, and stimulate our brain."

"That seems logical."

"Good. Now we go to Thomas' condition. Why is Thomas different from other people? Is it because he has a small brain? Is it because he has a different brain or an abnormal brain? What do you think?"

"I don't know." Seriously, I was out of my depths on how Thomas' brain had something to do with his behavior.

"Children like Thomas have parts of their brain that are taking time to develop. Even if you stimulate them all you want, each part of their brain develops differently from the others."

"Does that mean my son is more stupid than others?" I was getting angry at where this was leading. Was he accusing my son of being stupid?

"Nope. Far from it. Thomas may be brilliant in Mathematics or with words. He can be a genius for all we know. But that is just because one part of his brain is more developed than others. His intelligence in Mathematics is different from his capacity to think about other things for example. He may be good in that area, but poor in another. What is causing his current explosive behavior is that some parts of his brain fail to develop more maturely than other parts."

I was kind of set back at this. I just thought that to use your brain is just to solve problems in school or to think deeply about abstract concepts. Now, this person is telling me other areas of the brain that may be the cause of Thomas' misbehavior. At this point, I just wanted to ask, "So, how is this going to help Thomas?"

"The good thing about Thomas is that you can help him develop his brain if you know which particular part or function he is deficient in. The brain is a very plastic organ. Not in a material sense, but plastic means that it is able to develop and mature. When you train the brain, it can actually become more developed, catching up with other's normal development. Do you want to know what areas we can help Thomas?"

"Who wouldn't?" Now, this doctor is giving me some hope. But with a brain model, I'm not so sure if I can help Thomas grow his brain. But I wanted to trust this doctor, and hopefully, something good can come out of it.

"There are four sets of skills we can teach Thomas in order to help his brain develop fuller. These skills are trainable and can be developed through exercise and practice. Much like muscles in your arms, if you flex them enough, they will become bigger and more developed. If you don't practice them, they become deficient and you will see more of these explosions. I will discuss more of that after explaining these skills. But I just want to emphasize that these skills are necessary for life and that Thomas should develop them. These skills include: executive, language, emotional and social skills.

· ❤ · ❤ · ❤ · ❤ · ❤ ·

Executive Skills

The executive skills is a family of skills that help us perform higher functions of thinking. When you think of "executive," think of a boss that plans out what the different tasks are needed to run a business effectively, in this case, a human being. They are higher as compared to other forms of thinking because they resist impulsive thinking, helping us to make better choices than simply relying on our instincts. There are four subset of skills that any child needs to master in order to function well: inhibition, interference control, working memory and cognitive flexibility. I will try to explain each one as simply as I can.

Inhibition

The capacity to inhibit oneself refers to our ability to control our attention, thoughts, behaviors, emotions and express what is appropriate in a situation. This is the direct opposite of impulsive thinking, wherein the first thing we feel, we act on. When we have the capacity to restrain ourselves, we are able to think of other means of expressing ourselves in a manner that is appropriate. Let us look at examples to differentiate the two.

An officemate punches you in the face. What will you do?

Impulsive thinking: I feel so angry at the assault and I will punch that guy back.

Inhibitory thinking: I feel so angry at the assault. But is the situation appropriate? My boss and colleagues are all looking at me. I may get fired if I retaliate. So I will not fight now. But I will report the person to HR for disciplinary action.

In impulsive thinking, we simply act on what we feel at the moment which is anger that wants to get revenge. But in inhibitory thinking, we think of the consequences of our actions and decide on alternatives. There is still anger, but it was channeled differently into a more appropriate response. Inhibitory thinking is a mark of maturity because we are able to make better decisions when we don't act on our impulses alone. There is a recognition of the feeling, but the behavior is fitted to the appropriateness of that situation.

Interference Control

This refers to our capacity to concentrate. Our minds can only take in a few meaningful stimuli at a time, and the brain has to decide which ones are important and which ones to block. For example, you are at a party where there is a lot of noise. You are able to make meaningful conversation with another person by selectively blocking out the other sounds except for the voice of the person you are talking to. In this way, we are able to filter unnecessary or unimportant stimuli in order to concentrate our attention on what we feel is important. This can also be termed selective hearing, where we only want to hear things that we want to hear while blocking out other messages.

Interference control also refers to our ability to concentrate. There are many distractions around us as we are stimulated with a lot of sensations. When we deem an act to be important, we fend off all other thoughts and sensations aside in order to perform that act alone. This is important because we cannot get things done if we are constantly shifting our attention to other things instead of what is needed.

Even for adults, this is very difficult to perform because we are overstimulated. We have our gadgets and social media at hand. Even if we want to concentrate on a book we are studying or complete a problem set, we cannot help but feel tempted to text or send a message on our social media platforms. This represents a difficulty with interference control as we cannot focus our attention on tasks which we deem important.

Working Memory

The term 'memory' refers to things, objects, people, concepts, sensations, and ideas we remember. But unlike other forms of memories such as long-term memory, working memories refer to the things we continuously remember in our daily function. When I ask you what you do every day, you can immediately say, "I work in an office" or "I paint for a living." You are able to retrieve them quickly from your memory because you always use them. But if I ask, what was your first memory in school, it might take you a while to remember. You might say, "I remember my Grade 1 teacher" or "I had my first bike," which proves that you remember these events. But they take a long time to be retrieved from your memory because you don't use them every day.

Working memory is important because it helps us see connections in the things we normally sense daily. You see a street full of cars which are stopped. You use your memory and say that the traffic this afternoon is heavy. Therefore, you can choose another route that will enable you to take another course that is more efficient.

Working memory is also responsible for allowing you to see alternatives and factor in new information to old information to make good decisions. For example, you are going home after a long day at work. There is a car accident on your usual drive, blocking the path effectively. When you use your working memory, you take in the fact that the option of continuing in your usual route is not possible at the moment. So you think of other alternative routes to still get to your house. It may be passing through a different street just to bypass the blocked road. You are not going to wait all night on the road until it clears. With working memory, you see alternatives given new information. This stimulates your creativity to think of other possibilities while achieving the same goals.

Cognitive Flexibility

An important skill people need to learn is the capacity to shift perspectives. This can be in the form of an *interspatial* shift or an *interpersonal* shift. Interspatial shift refers to changing our perspectives in a spatial dimension. Suppose you want to place a sofa in a room. What would be the best place for the sofa? When you use cognitive flexibility, you can imagine the different locations of the sofa, from the top, the bottom, the sides, in reference to other objects. You can decide on an optimal position because you are flexible enough to see the different areas where you can put the sofa and place it in the most optimal place.

Interpersonal shift refers to our capacity to take in the perspective of another person. Suppose you really want to buy a new car this year. You are bent on buying it because you are just attracted to the shiny gloss of the car and the sophisticated design. But your husband is against it because you don't have enough budget for that year. When you take on the perspective of your husband, you are using cognitive flexibility. You are able to imagine the situation from another person's point of view and can see how your action can affect them.

Language Skills

This set of skills refers to our capacity to use language. This can be in the form of receptive or expressive language skills. As humans, we communicate mainly through speech. Hence, a good grasp of meaningful language is necessary to understand and to be understood by others.

Receptive skill refers to our ability to hear and make meaning out of what we hear. When a person tells us "apple," we are able to hear the different letters a-p-p-l-e, put them together and associate the sound, idea and image of the apple into one coherent data. This is then very important when we hear instructions, understand commands, read texts. If we understand what is needed from us, then we can act appropriately. If we have problems in receptive language skills, then we may not perform the expected action because we did not understand what was said.

Expressive language skill refers to how we communicate our ideas to others. This can be in the form of forming the words and expressing them by saying, "I want to go now," out loud. Or it can also be in the form of a higher functioning expression, such as choosing the word or expression which you really want to use. For example, you are feeling a strong emotion right now. Part of expression is choosing the right term to express that feeling. Is it anger or hate? Is it just annoyance or inconvenience? Is it loathing or vengeful? There is a whole range of vocabulary we need to learn in order for us to express that which we want to express.

There will be problems encountered when we have difficulty saying what we want to say. For example, you might not like the painting of one artist and you tell him, "I hate you." There is an incongruence between what you mean to say and feel and what you actually said. This can be a problem of not having enough vocabulary and also not knowing which vocabulary words are appropriate for the situation.

Emotional Skills

As humans, we have four basic emotions: glad, sad, mad, and afraid. There is a range of other emotions in each emotion, from the least to the most intense. Take, for example, happiness. We can feel content, peaceful, exuberant, or amused. But we can also feel elated, excited, ecstatic, or delirious. The situation, our personality, our meaning-making, will all affect the kind of emotion we are going to feel. When a person gives us a birthday cake, we normally feel happy. Perhaps, you may feel just as amused if you bake a cake every day and you are used to receiving cakes. Or you may feel ecstatic because that cake was given to you by a special loved one. Your individual experiences influence the intensity of the emotion you are going to feel.

In some cases, some feelings predominate over others in a lengthier period. Depression is an intense feeling of sadness that is pervasive throughout a number of weeks and months. Usually, feelings come and go, ebb and flow. But when the sadness remains for a long period of time, this warrants an investigation. Perhaps an imbalance of chemicals makes us feel so sad, angry, or anxious for a very long time.

Again, the emotion we feel has to be modulated by our executive skills. Yes, we feel angry because that is a legitimate feeling. But what we do to that feeling is a product of the executive function. Do we act on it impulsively or by controlling it? Can we think of alternatives that are more appropriate to the situation? Or is the feeling appropriate for the situation? If a car hits your car, it is certainly warranted that you get furious. But if somebody just happens to bump your hand slightly, is being furious warranted? Again, the executive function modulates the emotions we have and what we do with these.

Social Skills

The last set of skills integrates all the other skills together and brings the individual's thought processes, feelings and behaviors in relation to others. Part of socializing involves reading social cues, verbal and non-verbal signals that help us understand social interaction. When a person waves at you and smiles, you interpret that data and make sense of it. Is the person attacking me? Is the person expressing friendliness? From this interpretation, the individual then performs behaviors that are appropriate to the situation. The person can now respond with a wave and a smile or indifference because of the thought the other is a stranger. Whatever it is, these social skills help us interact with our social environment.

We use language to communicate with others. When we have a good set of receptive language skills, we can understand what is being said and what is being asked of us. A good set of expressive language skills allows us to communicate what we want to say and expect to get the results we want. Hence, our language skills become tested only through social interaction.

Our emotions are triggered by others. When we are given flowers on our birthday, we are happy. When we are confronted with a robber, we feel afraid. When someone passes away, we feel sad. Our emotions are affected by the circumstances outside of us. And in turn, we also affect others. When we help a grandmother walking down a street, she is grateful. When we are playing a prank on others, they feel annoyed or shocked. When we break up with a partner, it causes them pain. We are also capable of affecting others and triggering their emotions.

The executive function then moderates all these language and emotional skills to help us interact with others. We try to learn from others what they want to say and we formulate an appropriate response. We try to look at things from their perspective and try to feel what they are also feeling. This is called empathy, an important skill necessary for social function. We try to consider alternative courses of action that are socially acceptable and will benefit our purpose and also others. The executive function also allows us to set aside our own interests for the good of others. For example, a mother can forego buying an expensive piece of jewelry when her children need allowance for school. This capacity helps us become more mature persons when we are able to set aside personal agendas for the greater good.

You with me so far?"

That was quite a mouthful. But interesting nonetheless. "Yes, please continue."

The doctor goes on, "Now what happens in an explosion? This can simply be seen in the perspective of supply and demand. When the demand on a child is greater than his or her functional resources, then an explosion happens. It is as if the brain of the explosive child short-circuits and he just erupts. Too much cognitive functioning is asked of him and he does not have enough resources to process the information, hence, he explodes. It is important for us to know which skill is most affected. When we understand which skill, we can train the child to develop that skill more to prevent more explosions.

Let us look at some scenarios where a deficiency in each skill can lead to an eruption.

Executive Skill Example

A 10-year-old boy, Rudy, is going to school and is figuring out what to wear. His favorite color is blue and he always wore blue to school. When he opened his cabinet, there were no blue shirts on the shelves. He asked his mother, "Mom, I don't have blue shirts. I can't go to school." His mom replies, "Pick any shirt you like sweetie. I'll do the laundry tomorrow." But Rudy was insistent. He was so angry that he didn't have any blue shirt to wear. He began shouting aloud and threw a noisy tantrum.

In this situation, the demand was for Rudy to wear something for school. His usual preference was to wear blue shirts. But there was no blue shirt in sight. Rudy didn't have much working memory to think of other alternatives to blue shirts. He couldn't think of wearing white or green or any other colored shirt.

He also felt very angry at the thought of not having a blue shirt. It may seem trivial for some, but for Rudy, his anger was really intense. Instead of holding back his feelings, he acted on it. With such great demand and few resources, Rudy exploded. This is a classic example of a deficiency in executive skills.

Language Skill Example

Amy kept on pointing at the cupboards above and was whimpering. Her dad noticed her and asked, "Honey, what is it that you want?" Amy just kept on pointing at the cupboards, expecting her father to know. "I don't understand you. What do you want?" But Amy could not say what she wanted to say and simply pointed at the cupboard. Her father then began to go over the items on the cupboard.

 "Is it this jar of cookies?"

"No!"

"Is it this bottle of milk?"

"No!"

"Is it this green mug?"

"No" and Amy fell into pieces, just whimpering inconsolably.

In this case, we can see the frustration in Amy in communicating what she wanted. The demand was that she wanted an item on the cupboard. But her vocabulary resources were scarce. She didn't have the words to name that object, describe it even, or simply point at it exactly. Her father is not a mind reader and hence relied on language heavily. He couldn't interpret what she was pointing at. The demand exceeded Amy's resources and she exploded.

Emotional Skill Example

"Who took my robot?" Bryan was adamant about finding who the culprit was. Bryan was sure he placed it on the table but he couldn't find it. He did not remember it at that time, but he actually placed the train near the television. He went to another room for a while. On his return, he couldn't find where he placed his robot.

"Somebody took my robot! You better give it back or else..." Bryan threatened.

"Honey, maybe you just placed it somewhere else. Try looking for it," his mother offered.

"I think Cindy took it. I will really beat her up for getting my toy!" There was a dangerous tone to Bryan's threats.

"Honey, you better stop that. Your baby sister is sleeping upstairs. She couldn't possibly take it." Her mother knew there was impending danger.

"No, somebody took my robot!" and Bryan began kicking away at the sofa chairs and pillows. It took around thirty minutes for his anger to dissipate until they found his robot lying next to the television.

In this case, clearly, Bryan was overwhelmed with his feeling of anger. First, the intensity was not appropriate for the situation. Threatening to kick his sister over a lost toy is not a healthy expression of feelings. Next, the feeling overpowered Bryan. His executive skills did not allow him to set that aside and think of other alternatives, other places where he might have placed the toy. The demand exceeded Bryan's capacity to confront the loss; hence he exploded.

Social Skill Example

Rebecca was patiently falling in line in the cafeteria. It was lunch and the menu was Rebecca's favorite ham sandwich and cheese. She didn't care much for the salad, but at least there was ham. She was quite close to the counter when a boy cut her on the line and started getting food from the lunch lady. Rebecca was furious. The next thing she knew, she was hitting the boy with the silver tray. Rebecca got her revenge, but she also got detention.

In this case, we can see that Rebecca was following the social order of falling patiently in line. She was right. But when a person cut her off, she knew that the boy was not following social rules. She was so angry that she kept following the rules while others didn't. But she couldn't control her anger. She didn't think of other possibilities like telling the boy off or telling the lunch lady to reprimand the boy. She immediately took action. The demand was too much for her resources and Rebecca just exploded.

These four scenarios are just some examples of how explosive children tick off. It is a simple formula of demands exceeding resources. We cannot control the demand because things just happen to us. But we can do something about the resources. We can actually train our kids to develop these skills so that they have enough resources to respond to any situation in an appropriate manner. This is where therapy and your parenting begins to matter."

I don't know about you, but that was a pretty good explanation to me. I began to look at the plastic brain model and just marvel at how complex it is. It's not as intimidating as I first thought of it. Now, I began to respect this wonderful organ that controls our behaviors, thoughts, and actions. And I guess what the doctor said also applies to us adults. When we 'lose it,' we also exceed our capacity to meet the demand. When a driver is cut by another car, the usual reaction is to honk your horn or even just express anger inside the car. But when you bump the other car or even threaten to shoot the other driver, the emotions are inappropriate in intensity and the actions are not appropriate for the cause. The executive functional skills of some adults seriously need development. Hence, some kids grew up to become explosive adults themselves. In a way, this book is not just for parents who have explosive kids, but it is also for all of us who have felt explosive ourselves.

Chapter 4

Predicting an Eruption

· ♥ · ♥ · ♥ · ♥ · ♥ ·

"Look mom, I made you heart pancakes!" Louisa excitedly told me.

"Thank you Louisa, that's very sweet of you."

"I also made pancakes for Dad, Grandma, Sarah, Bobby and little Reese," she continued.

"Alright, call everyone down for breakfast."

Louisa called out her siblings and they started arriving at the table, taking their places.

"Mom, Bobby is sitting in my chair," Louisa pointed out.

"It's alright honey, take another seat."

"But that is my chair. I want that chair." Louisa was becoming worked up.

Little Bobby looked at me and said, "Mom, can I sit here?"

At that point, I just didn't care where they sat as long as they kept the peace. "Children, just sit where you want to sit ok. Let's just eat breakfast."

"But Bobby is sitting in my chair. I want my chair back!" Louisa was adamant. Bobby chimed in, "But I'm already eating breakfast."

"I don't care. I made those pancakes and I want my chair back!" And Louisa throws her pancake at Bobby.

This is an anecdote from one of our new attendees in our support group. And no matter how many times you hear an eruption story, you will never cease to be baffled at the littlest things that set explosive children off. Whether it is a favorite seat or a favorite shirt that was taken from them, they are bound to wreak havoc at the slightest inconvenience. They may be sweet at one moment and then fuming in another.

Eruptions are never beautiful. The noise, the kicking, the throwing of objects, the breaking of toys, the public embarrassment, and the anger triggered inside us is always ugly to behold. But the only beautiful thing in eruptions is that they are actually predictable. Like volcanoes impending to erupt, explosive children are actually easy to track when they will burst.

· ♥ · ♥ · ♥ · ♥ · ♥ ·

Patterns of Explosions

My first advice to all parents who have explosive children: track their triggers. Know what exactly sets them off. Take a journal with you and in a span of a week, recall and chronicle each eruption your child has. What were the circumstances surrounding the eruption? What were the specific words, actions, gestures, things that were present and prodded your child to have a fit? By listing these down, you are going to have an idea of what things will trigger your child. You have to see patterns of behavior, connections between events and repetitive tropes that connect all these eruptions. You will have a bigger picture then and have a handle on how to manage your explosive child.

Routine

Explosive children tend to be protective of routines. They have their own ways of eating, drinking, sleeping, playing, and studying. They may have a certain ritual when brushing their teeth. They may have a particular order to eating food that is given to them. When they are studying, the books must be placed in a certain way in respect to the pens and the notebooks. When they go to school, they strictly follow a certain path. There are allowances for some variation, but more or less, they stick to a regular routine of things.

And this is very calming for them. In their mind, a routine presents a certain control over events. They like the routine because they want things to be predictable. It may be boring for some, but for them, this is ideal. The more the routine is repeated, the calmer they become. They are very protective of routines.

You will see this importance when a routine is disrupted. As in the case in the beginning of the chapter, Louisa had a certain seat she was rather fond of. Perhaps she liked the position of that chair, or she just got used to sitting there after a long time. It calms her down when she is sitting in that particular chair. And so when Bobby gets her chair, the routine is disrupted. Louisa explodes because her routine was not followed.

Disruption of routines is part of the executive skills we should be learning. The mind is already trained to look for patterns. The mind wants everything to be the same, occurring in a particular way. But the mind should also be flexible enough to accommodate certain changes in the routine. This is working memory expanding wherein new information is added to old information. There is room for choosing alternatives because routines are challenged.

But with explosive children, their capacity to accommodate new information and new routines is undeveloped. They are not used to another way of doing things. And so they will tend to resist change by throwing a tantrum. The only way you can calm them down is if you give in to what they want. But if you indulge them in their routines, then their executive skills are not developed. They will have difficulty in the future when things don't fall into a routine.

Possessiveness

One of the first words an explosive child will use a lot is 'mine.' That toy is mine. That pillow is mine. That bottle is mine. They are able to distinguish between what is theirs and what belongs to others. This is a good skill because they can identify objects which are important to them.

In the developing brain, the sense of the ego is very prominent. As a newborn, we tend only to look at the world in reference to us. Growing up, we think that the world revolves around us, strengthening the self-identity of the ego. And slowly, we realize that there are other people like us. First, there is mom, who gives us our milk. Then there is dad, who carries us sometimes and changes our diapers. There are extended families. The more we encounter other people, the more we realize that there are other beings aside from ourselves. And this is a healthy progression from self to others.

In explosive children, they tend to be stuck in their own worlds. There is some recognition of others and their possessions and feelings. But the primary references are still themselves. This may be due to a deficiency in social skills or cognitive flexibility which is putting yourself in the perspective of others. But explosive children tend to be possessive of their things. If you give them a toy, then that object is theirs. If you take it away, they will cry and bawl because they don't recognize that it used to be yours. If they have a favorite item missing, they will be restless until that object is returned. These physical objects give them a sense of peace and calm that they have possessions they can control.

Once you are able to plot which are the common triggers and patterns of behavior of your explosive child, you can now anticipate the pattern of eruption. We can classify these events in terms of stages. Normal, pre-explosion, explosion and post-explosion. I feel that these are important stages to note because there are specific interventions for each.

Normal

This is the child's usual state. Here, they are most agreeable and sweet, free from any signs of an explosion. They are able to think well and can be reasoned with. They may be engaging in cooperative play with others or in solitary activity. You can talk to them in regular conversation and they appear to be responsive, even genial. This is the stage where the child is really at their best, showcasing how they are striving to be agreeable to everyone. It's tempting to call this 'the calm before the storm' because of the seemingly benign nature of this stage. The explosion might be the more dramatic reference point, but the normal stage is the ideal stage where your child should aim to be at. You want to prolong this stage. You hope that the child may hopefully achieve a permanent stage of normalcy.

This is important to determine because the normal stage is where you can do the most interventions. When they are most calm, most collected and most agreeable, they are also most able to reason out well. This is where you can talk with them to discuss how they can help themselves change their thinking and behavior. This might trigger another explosion when you start to discuss. But you have to start that conversation at some point, and this is the best opportunity. After a while, they will get used to anticipating 'the talk' when they are in their normal stage. At that point, you can make it a habit to really engage them in a conversation about enhancing their skills.

Pre-explosion

The pre-explosion are the events leading to the actual explosion. It's the pre-game, the collection of signs pointing out to a possible eruption. This is characterized by a number of factors. It begins with an index event. Something happened. You might not know it when it is happening, but a trigger is setting the child off. It can be a missing toy, an argument with a sibling, a routine that was not followed, an interruption of their study habits, a social cue they failed to read. Whatever it is, there was an incident. Explosive kids don't explode spontaneously; they were provoked.

Next, you will note changes in the speech pattern of the child leading to the explosion. The voice is slowly increasing in pitch, tone, and speed. It is not yet at the screaming point, but there is a definite urgency to the voice's tone. The content of the speech is also important. They may or may not be able to verbalize the incident or what they want to say. They may complain to you about what happened but they may also fail to specify what exactly happened. This is an expressive language problem that you must address in the normal stage. You will hear familiar words like 'that is mine' or 'I want it now,' signs of egoistic reference. Again, they feel attacked, thinking that their environment is ganging up on them and want to insist on their interest.

There is also a change in their behavior already happening. You can see that they are physically agitated with the frequency of movements. They may be more restless, as seen in their legs, and they would like to pace to and fro to relieve that anxiety. The facial expression is also a cue. They will really show that they are angry or irritated at the event.

This stage can be variable in terms of length. For some, the pre-explosion may take a while and can even dissipate when they are given what they want. But this does not mean that you should always accede to their wishes just to end the explosion. There is still value in teaching them how to handle their emotions. But this stage can also be very abrupt. With one trigger, it can be a matter of minutes before they explode, reducing the pre-explosion phase. The trigger and the mental preparedness of the child can determine the length of the pre-explosion stage.

Is there a way to terminate this stage? As we have said, giving in to them will surely cut off the explosion. Hurray for you because you avoided the fireworks. That can work some of the time when you are really just buying time. There are times that you can give in to them just to let them know that you acknowledge their requests when it is warranted. But do not make this a habit just to avoid explosions. You have to teach your kids that what they are feeling is legitimate, but they can act on it in a more appropriate and timely manner.

There can be some emergency interventions at this point. Children can still be reasoned out at this stage and it is important for you not to tire out in engaging them in a meaningful conversation. Yes, you may be tired and just want to get over it. There are times when you also just want to insist on your own way. But there is more value in letting the child learn and develop his or her emotional skills even in an impending explosion. Test how far they can go when they reason. There are times when they just don't want to think of other possibilities or take the perspective of the other. Reason out with them anyway. You know that they are going to explode, but at least you have challenged them to think more. This is an exciting stage to teach your child, so don't miss the opportunity just because the explosion is ugly.

There are also pre-emptive measures you can take when you think that this will lead to an explosion and that the child has a tendency to be violent. You can take away objects that they can throw or break. You can tell your other children to leave the premises. Or you can simply isolate your explosive child in a safe environment where they can detonate without hurting anyone else. You have to ensure the safety of everyone when the explosion happens.

Explosion

And so we come to the climax of the event, the explosion. This is the ugly event that ensues when the demands far exceed their mental resources. Each child will have a particular way of exploding. The list is endless and you can definitely add your own:

The Screamers

They will scream at the top of the voices which can be heard by neighbors and nearby people. They can keep on screaming until they become hoarse.

The Gushers

They will simply cry relentlessly and crumple to the floor. They can be inconsolable and keep on crying for hours as though they suffered a grave injury.

The Curser

These children tend to shout out expletives which they either learned at home, in school, with their friends, on social media. This is particularly stressful because younger children may be exposed to this and also learn how to curse

The Thrower

They will fling any object within reach. This can be a toy, a vase, a bottle, plates on the table, your cellphone, anything. This is a red flag in terms of safety because they may hurt themselves or others. They can break windows or other fixtures.

The Boxer

These are the more dangerous children who can be physically aggressive. They will try to punch or kick you if you try to contain them. The tendency is for you to fight back so prepare for bruises and cuts.

The Walker

These kids just want to escape the scene of conflict so they usually walk-out. They want to go to a calm place and detonate on their own. Let them if you know that they are going to a safe place. But be wary if they walk out on their own to some place you don't know. You might end up searching for them all over. Some even disappear for days on end causing much distress in the family.

The Vengeful

These kids may not appear violent and aggressive when they explode. But they have a tendency to exact revenge at another time. They will dismiss the incident and find a more opportune moment to strike. If their toy was taken from them, they could take another kid's toys. If they feel hurt at your scolding, they can get back at you by taking your things or anything that may annoy you. So, be wary about these kids because it is hard to catch them when they are exacting their revenge.

· ♥ · ♥ · ♥ · ♥ · ♥ ·

You might get the impression that explosive kids are all bad. I'm not saying that at all. I think that these kids are really misguided and they don't know how to vent out their emotions properly. They need your guidance when they erupt, so don't think that they are bad kids. I have merely presented the range of behaviors they may exhibit when they explode.

The first consideration when a kid is on eruption mode is to secure the safety of everyone. There is a strong tendency for destruction to persons and property, so you have to make sure that everyone is safe. If they are exploding, it should be in an environment where they cannot hurt themselves or others. Put away any objects that can be a cause of damage. They can cry and roll on the floor as they want as long as the area is safe.

Second, be very conscious of your own feelings. Their anger can trigger yours. It is really very frustrating and distressing to see a child throw a tantrum. They will bring out the worst in you. If you have tried all methods to appease them and are still inflexible, you might also reach your boiling point. Remember that you are the adult here, more capable of understanding the situation and managing your feelings. If you think that you will reach a point where you can hurt the child, then it is better for you to leave the premises and calm down. If you are going to speak out your anger, you might regret the things you may say. So if you have reached your boiling point, have another adult take over the situation until you are in a better position. If you really can't leave at the moment, just keep quiet. Your calmness will affect the kid. It may even cause him to be calm because his antics are not taking any effect on you. Remember that this is your kid at their worst. It is at this point that they need you to be at your best because they are weaker than you. I know it is hard, but it will take some practice.

Can you intervene at this point? The usual tendency is just to give in to the kid's requests as in the pre-explosion. That is the easiest solution and may reverse the explosion. And yet, it is not the most ideal because you are not helping him make better decisions. You just want to get it over with without actually using the situation to your advantage. It is a teaching moment presenting itself to you, so grab it.

You can simply let the kid be. If they want to shout, let them shout. If they want to cry, let them cry. After a while, they will become tired. When they see that you are still calm, they will also calm down. Then you are going to move to the post-explosion phase. But during the drama, you just have to let them express all that anger and irritation out.

They are not optimal for reasoning at this point. They may be so consumed with their own emotions that they will not entertain any reason. Just let them express all that in a safe environment. They are children, after all, and are still growing in their capacity to hold their emotions. It is difficult to be in an explosion, but you just have to trust that they need to undergo this painful process. You can constantly assure them that you feel for them and that they can talk to you when they are a bit calmer. But you just have to endure this phase until it passes.

Post-explosion

After the drama has passed, the child will most likely be tired at this point. They have cried all their tears and have exhausted all their energy kicking and thrashing around. Good for them if they got what they want. Good for you if you stood your ground. But it is actually no good for everyone because you feel tired after all the action has transpired. It is at this point that you can reach out to your child. They are at their most vulnerable at this point. You can invite them to talk about what happened so that you can process their feelings and thoughts. But also respect them if they don't want to talk yet. Maybe they need some alone time to process what happened on their own. They just feel so tired that they want some calmness and solitude. Respect their space.

This stage can proceed either to the normal stage or to another explosive stage. If they are triggered anew or the previous episode was not resolved fully, they can launch into another round of explosion. But most of them simply proceed to the normal stage. What is important is that they learn from the situation. Don't let the opportunity pass by where you don't get to process what happened. If they are a bit calmer and in the normal stage, that is the best time to talk with them. If you don't process their feelings, then the episode will repeatedly happen without being conscious of their own patterns.

Also, look out for yourself in the post-explosion stage. Check your feelings. Do you also feel exhausted? Are you still full of anger and irritation about the situation? Do you feel sad about the explosions which you feel have no improvement? It's ok. You have to be true to what you are feeling. As much as you want to care for your child, you also have to care for yourself. During the post-explosion, check your feelings and see if you are still in a good position to teach your kid.

These stages are largely culled from my experience of taking care of Thomas and his explosions. When I listen to other parents reporting about their own children's explosions, I kind of outline the story in these stages. It is important to talk about the normal stage because it is not fair to the kid just to dwell in the weakest moments. Children want to be the best that they can be. So we should never highlight the explosion. We should support their normal best selves and use the explosions as a guide as to how far they are still from their best versions. It is this

distance that we need to close when we begin our approach
to pushing our explosive kids to become their best selves.

Chapter 5

The Shifting Table

· ♥ · ♥ · ♥ · ♥ · ♥ ·

The heart of wisdom I want to share with you lies in the unique approach I have used with Thomas. This is a product of many sessions with various therapists who have guided my family. I have tried this method and I can see that Thomas has improved a lot because of this. I have refined over the years and I have shared it with my fellow support group members. I feel that is the most loving approach we can use to tame the fire in our children. It is very effortful and will require a lot of patience for everyone involved in taking care of your children. There will be times that you will have to confront your own issues, but focus on making your children better. I assure you that the results are worth all the labor you will invest. Thomas isn't perfectly obedient and agreeable all the time, even after years of doing this method with him. But he has grown to be more in control of his emotions and makes an effort to really think about his actions.

The Table

The table is an imaginary setting where you can encounter your child in a meaningful manner. It must be a safe place first and foremost, a place where you can both be calm and collected. If there is still a lot of noise, distractions, or intense emotions, then no reasonable conversation can happen. You have to both be ready to reach out to one another, and a safe space will make that possible.

It is an invitation to a conversation where both you and your child can talk about issues that concern the both of you. It usually starts with "Can we talk?" from you and allows the child to be led to the table. Do not rush going to the table or immediately starting a conversation. The table should be made ready in a leisurely manner. This allows you and the child to relax and talk more reasonably about their behavior. You can start in silence, one that invites the child to also speak out and not be intimidated by an adult. In silence, they will feel that something is important because it is not your usual self to be silent around them.

When you approach the table, make sure that the child understands that this is an event that is important to you and to them.

The Shifting Table is a place of negotiation. You are going to talk to your kid because you want something from them and they want to obtain something, not necessarily from you. Realize that they don't want to talk. They don't want to exert any effort to change what is easy and convenient for them. They will try to bend you to their will and so a negotiation with them is effortful. And so the kid will not welcome the table or any conversation to change their behavior readily. The task of initiating an invitation to the table comes largely from you. If you are also as reluctant to make any meaningful conversation with them in a negotiation, then the table is pointless. You can't just force the kid to do what you want. But at the table, there is an effort of both parties to hear each other's side.

How do we approach the table? How do we start any conversation about changing a thought or a behavior we feel is misdirected? It is good for us to know what the dynamics of effective conversation are. The Greek word 'dialogue' is a good illustration of this. The word 'dialogue' comes from the Greek 'di' which means 'two' and 'logos' which means 'word'. A dialogue is about two people engaging in an exchange of words. There are three basic perspectives that we need to be aware of when we approach the table.

Me Perspective

"Parents know what is best for their child." If you subscribe to this, then you are using the 'Me' perspective. Of course, you have a personal agenda. You want your kid to follow your command because you think that this is the best for them. You have committed mistakes before and you don't want that to happen to your child. And so you feel strongly that your perspective, which is bigger and more comprehensive than theirs, should be followed. Your brain is much more developed through years of experience and interaction. Therefore you are in a better position to teach what is right. Plus, you have the advantage of size, authority and resources to enforce your commands. At any point, it will be easy to bend the child to your will arbitrarily because you can. "I am your parent and you can't do anything."

But this 'me' perspective is not just about power dynamics. It is also about love. You love your son or daughter so much that you just want them to have the best in life. Your goal is not to be a hindrance to your child's happiness but to enable them to achieve the best kind of happiness there is. It is not simply saying 'no' to every child's request that makes you a strong parent. These decisions of permitting or disallowing comes from a genuine desire for the good of the other. We want the child to be protected and safe and so we try to prevent anything that will harm them. The child may not understand that at times because they will feel that you are simply policing them, making their lives complicated and miserable. But all your decisions, commands and requests come from a deep love for your children.

Them Perspective

The child will simply look after himself. They are still in the process of becoming mature, both in physical and mental capacity. Their minds are still turned inwards, to making sure that they are well-fed, happy and independent to do whatever they want. They like to explore and are curious about everything. They want to try new things, but they also feel comfortable in routines and in what is familiar to them. Attention is fleeting because they want to be stimulated with as much sensory information as they can. Children want to be as happy as they possibly can. And they will resort to all sorts of antics to preserve this happiness, whether it is through pleasing the adult or crying their way out. What works for them to achieve their happiness, they will continue to do. If sitting quietly and waiting for their turn will get them their marshmallow, then they will try to wait until the end. If threatening and thrashing around will get them their marshmallow, then they will perform their ballistic maneuvers. What works is repeated.

Are they selfish then? Selfishness is a word we use when there is a conscious decision to choose the self, knowing the perspective of the other. Hence, a child cannot be seen as selfish. Yes, they have their own self-interest at heart. But they also are just developing the capacity to think and feel for the other person. The consciousness of another person, also feeling the same feelings as me, is a mark of maturity which they will have to go through. Don't take it personally when children seem to be selfish. It's just that they are not yet developed enough.

Us Perspective

The most crucial and necessary perspective is the *Us Perspective*. The 'us' refers to a mutual satisfaction of both parties– your interests and concerns are addressed as well as the child's. This perspective benefits both parties in some acceptable manner. There is respect for the feelings and concerns of the child. But there is also a recognition of the value of the adult's proposition. This perspective can only come if there is both a capacity to be aware of the concerns, thought, feelings of the other and a willingness to compromise. It is easy to assume that the adult is aware of the feelings and concerns of the child. But this is not true all of the time. Like children, some parents also only think about their concerns rather than making an effort to reach out. Therefore, the *Us Perspective* entails an effort from both parties to think and feel for the other and to hold the possibility of not doing their wills in order to consider the good of the other. So much mental resource is needed then to arrive at a mutually satisfying decision.

Is there such a thing then as a perfectly and equally satisfying decision? Not all the time. Think of an *Us Perspective* as a range of possibilities between your concern and their concern. The balance is optimal if it is right smack at the middle, with both parties equally benefitting. But in real life, some decisions favor the other person. It isn't exactly in the middle, but it may lean towards one party more than the other. And that's ok. Each party must simply state what points which are non-negotiable for them are. Yes, I can give in to your wish, but I cannot accept it if it crosses the line.

Hence, the table is necessary to settle that *Us Perspective*. It is a negotiation where parties will arrive at a decision that they can both accept. For example, your child wants to go to the shopping mall right now to buy toys. That is his perspective. You are still busy at the moment and can only take him and next month. A perfect compromise would be to go to the mall between your proposed dates. But as in all negotiations, you can compromise another date which is acceptable for you both. That is the point where you have reached an *Us Perspective*. The child gets to go to the shopping mall and you are able to do your work and accede to his wishes at an appropriate time.

Is the *Us Perspective* decision all important? I am telling you that the results of the negotiation are not as important as the process of arriving at it. I don't care if you go to the mall now, next week, next month or next year. It will matter to the child because he really wants it. But the more important value is taking the effort to meet the other, to take the perspective of the other even for a moment. More than arriving at decisions, you have to teach your kid to respect and love the process of making decisions. When you are able to reason out with them, then you will feel happy that your child is attempting to understand where you are coming from, what you are feeling. They will also feel validated when they feel that you also care for them, that you respect their concerns. You may end up actually just following the child's decision at times. But because you went through the process of negotiating, considering alternatives, taking the perspective of the other, then that decision becomes mutually satisfying. Arriving at the *Us Perspective* is an art that must be practiced in order to perfect. And when you engage in meaningful and loving negotiation, then the decisions don't actually matter.

Do we use the *Us Perspective* all the time? To think about the other is very effortful and will require a lot of resources from all parties. This can be a tiring process if you have to do it over and over again for the most mundane and trivial of decisions. It is easier to fall back into a *Me Perspective* just to get it over with. The child will really insist on *Them Perspective* because it is convenient. The answer will really depend on the child's developing mental capacity. As we have said in the previous chapter, their brain is still in the process of maturing. The executive, language, emotional and social skills are developed through time. And so you have to adopt the perspective appropriate for the age of the child.

For babies, you don't ask them if they want milk or not. There is no sense in negotiating because they don't have the capacity to verbalize what they want, to engage in any meaningful conversation. Hence, you apply the *Me Perspective* at this stage. You want your child to be nourished and safe, so you have to insist on your perspective for their good.

But at around the age of two to three, the child becomes more independent. They are able to blurt out two to three word sentences. They can express a variety of emotions.

They are exposed to family, playmates and strangers all enriching their social interactions. All of these stimuli help their brain to develop and their mental skills to mature. It is at this stage that you can already apply the *Us Perspective*. By engaging them in a negotiation, you are helping them develop themselves. You might think that they are too young for this. Maybe, you still need to cling on to the *Me Perspective* for a while until they go to school. But part of the *Us Perspective* is recognizing the child as also capable of making unique decisions, respecting their thoughts and feelings. Yes, they may not make the best decision. But their feelings are still valid and should be recognized. Hence, I recommend using this *Us Perspective* early on whenever you feel that the child can already engage in meaningful conversation. It is a language that will determine the perspective to be used.

Is there room then for a *Them Perspective*? As they are growing up, the *Us Perspective* should be enforced more prominently. The *Us Perspective* also considers the concern of the child, taking into account the *Them Perspective*. You feel for your child. You are hurt when they are hurt. You feel concerned when they are angry. You try to put yourself in their situation. And in some cases, it is more prudent to give in to the child's wishes. But this cannot proceed without undergoing the process of negotiating. "I feel you but I also have a point." "You want to go to the mall so bad, but I am also busy at the moment." "You don't want to come to grandma's house, but we will feel bad if you don't." Ultimately, we need to emphasize the big role of the *Us Perspective* because the 'them' is already natural to them and need not be taught.

And even as adults, we may have different perspectives. We recognize that each one has their own opinions, values, and convictions. But we see a lot of tension and disagreements among adults because we have not mastered the art of negotiation. We have not been practicing the *Us Perspective* too well, insisting only that our opinion is what matters. We fail to make an effort to arrive at mutually satisfactory decisions, courses of action that will benefit all parties. I want to emphasize the *Us Perspective* on children because we want to raise a generation that is willing to cooperate and not just to compete.

When you are handling the child in the pre-explosion, explosion, and post-explosion phase, it is really difficult not to take the *Us Perspective*. We just want to get it over with so either we insist on our own way or give in to the child. But as I have emphasized, it is not about the decision. It is about the process of coming together and making an effort to understand the other. There is greater value in recognizing the other's concern and being willing to make adjustments. It is in the normal stage where we can process more of their feelings and thoughts so that we can change their behavior. Always insist that the *Us Perspective* is crucial to their development, enabling them to have more mental resources to draw from and address the demand. Don't be afraid of the steam and the destruction the explosion may spew forth. What is important is that you have created an opportunity for them to learn and develop new skills.

Chapter 6

Approaching the Table

· ❤ · ❤ · ❤ · ❤ · ❤ ·

"Can we talk?" I wasn't one to start conversations but I thought that my son John needed me to make the first move.

"I don't want to talk with you. I'm so mad you won't let me go for soccer practice." John said.

"But I need you to be in the house. Your sister has to have someone watching over her while I am making repairs in the house." I reasoned out.

"My teammates depend on me. I feel happy when I am with them. And you're taking that happiness away from me." John was inflexible.

"But John, you can always go to soccer practice next week. I just need you to be here while I am doing something." I pointed out.

"I don't want to stay. I will leave the house." he threatened.

"Don't make it difficult for me. You stay here or you're grounded." I raised my voice.

"That's unfair!" John was shouting.

"But you have to understand Daddy is doing a lot of things. Buddy, I just need you to stay just for today until we can sort things out. Can you do that for me?"

"No. I'm leaving whether you want it or not." John was pushing me to my limit.

This is another anecdote from a father in our support group. He has a son, John, who appears very inflexible. The dad is divorced and has to take care of the children on his own. He relies on John to take care of a younger sibling. But John has been used to getting his way. He knows that if he just stood his ground, he will get what he wants. They didn't seek any therapy at all because John's father felt that his behavior was typical of his age. But I finally convinced them to seek some help when I noticed that John's inflexibility was already straining his dad's patience and resources. They were able to make some progress but only after several sessions.

This conversation can serve as our jumping point for our approach to *The Shifting Table*. We have established that it is important to invite the child to a conversation. They will resist it because they don't want to make an effort to think. But, it is good for you to teach them to develop new skills. You can start with 'Can we talk?' so as to invite the child and alert him that you are approaching the table. This can be in the normal, pre or post-explosion stage, anytime that the child feels calm enough to be reasoned out with. When you have opened up the conversation, how exactly do you go about approaching *The Shifting Table*?

I propose a simple framework for developing your conversation. Simply follow the format of MIRROR, PROPOSE, DECIDE. It's a simple method of letting your explosive child let out their feelings and consider possibilities to make the best decision benefitting both of you. We will go through each part and how you can apply it with your child.

· ♥ · ♥ · ♥ · ♥ · ♥ ·

Mirror

Any conversation will have to recognize the feelings of both persons involved. The child is explosive at the moment. There are intense feelings of anger, rage, irritation, sadness, and frustration, all at the same time. This causes them to behave in such an inflexible manner. You have to be aware of these feelings and recognize that they are valid. Emotions are far more powerful and pervasive in affectation rather than reason or logic. The child will not be able to reason out well when they are still consumed by their emotions. Therefore, if you want to make them think, you have to address what they are feeling first. When a child feels that their emotions are recognized, they are more predisposed to listen to you. They will feel safe that they are valued even if their feelings seem trivial to you.

The way we approach feelings is through mirroring. Just like a mirror, you have to reflect on what it is that they are feeling. In the case of John and his father, the conversation went:

Dad: Can we talk?

John: I don't want to talk with you. I'm so mad you won't let me go for soccer practice.

Here, we can clearly see that John is mad. The feeling that needs to be recognized is anger. Instead of going directly to what he wanted, the father should have addressed that anger first. He can phrase it as:

Dad: Can we talk?

John: I don't want to talk with you. I'm so mad you won't let me go for soccer practice.

Dad: You're mad that I didn't let you go for soccer practice.

Just that simple line, when said sincerely, can really go a long way. You want to make the child feel that their anger is legitimate, and that you accept that. Mirroring may look like just repeating what is said, like an echo. But this is important because you want to use their own words, not just yours. There is going to be a problem when you start assuming that they feel a particular emotion when they are not. You feel that they are angry, but actually, they are just disappointed. You assume that they are irritable, but they are just afraid. When you mirror their words, you are avoiding that mistake and letting the child know that you know exactly how they feel. Don't just say the word monotonously and out of routine. Really mean it when you say you empathize with them. Be sincere that you can understand what they are feeling.

A follow up to this conversation can be:

Dad: I'm sorry that you're mad at my decision. But I also feel worried for your sister.

There are two parts to this. The dad actually said, "I'm sorry." Now, we have to clarify what we mean when we say, "I'm sorry." When we say that, we are not just referring to an acceptance of our fault as in the case, "I'm sorry I hurt you." It does not mean that you are admitting that you were in the wrong and now correcting things. Rather, saying "I'm sorry" means that you recognize the bad feeling in the other person. You are empathizing that the other is not feeling well, or has encountered a misfortune. "I'm sorry" is our attempt to reach out to the other's negative feelings. So don't be afraid to say "I'm sorry" because you think that it is a sign of weakness. It is merely a recognition of the bad feelings in another.

The last part is really a sharing of your own emotions. If they are able to express themselves, you should also make them aware that their actions affect you. This is already appealing to their executive and emotional skills, specifically cognitive flexibility. You are asking the kid to place themselves in your position and feel what you are feeling. They may be uninterested in acknowledging your feelings. But still, you should say this. Let them know and feel that they are not the only ones with feelings.

So the format of the mirroring is really: Their emotion →
I'm sorry → my emotion. Both parties must acknowledge
sincerely how they are affected by the situation. No
rational conversation can proceed when the emotions are
not addressed initially. When the heart has calmed down,
then you can proceed with stimulating the child's rational
decision-making skills.

Propose

This is where you literally put your cards on the table. Take
time to ask what they want to happen and also propose
to them what you want to happen. Look for overlaps
or similarities in your proposals that can be avenues for
compromise. Recognize first that they have a concern, an
actual course of action they want to pursue. It can be the
silliest of things or the most trivial. But let them identify
that. There is a bigger problem when they actually don't
know what they want to do or happen. It becomes a
language problem when they are not able to verbalize their
wants. So let them practice saying what they want to say.

In turn, also propose your own take on the matter. There
is a problem that you need to resolve and you have a way
to address it. State your proposal clearly so the child can
understand how your way is better than theirs. Sometimes,
it is just a matter of explaining yourself clearly that will do

the trick. If you just insist on "I am your parent, follow me." then the child misses out on the rationality of the decision. They must see that your proposal has some sense.

So in the previous conversation, there was an attempt to explain both of their sides. Let's see how well they were able to present their cases.

		Bottom Line
Dad:	But I need you to be in the house. Your sister has to have someone watching over her while I am making repairs in the house.	You have to stay in the house for your sister.
John:	My teammates depend on me. I feel happy when I am with them. And you're taking that happiness away from me.	I want to go to soccer practice.
Dad:	But John, you can always go to soccer practice next week. I just need you to be here while I am doing something.	You can go next week.
John:	I don't want to stay. I will leave the house.	I want to go now.
Dad:	Don't make it difficult for me. You stay here or you're grounded.	You're grounded.
John:	That's unfair!	You're being unfair.
Dad:	But you have to understand Daddy is doing a lot of things. Buddy, I just need you to stay just for today until we can sort things out. Can you do that for me?	Understand me.
John:	No. I'm leaving whether you want it or not.	I don't want to follow your request.

I have provided my own interpretation of the conversation in the bottom line column. If I were to reduce that conversation, the bottom line preserves the essence of what is actually being said. When we look at the bottom line, no attempt to listen to the other was taking place. They were simply interested in their own agenda by evidence of the repetitive words like 'I,' 'me.'

The father said a proposal. He wanted John to stay in the house. That is clear. But he isn't clear how long John has to stay. Does John have to stay in the house all week, all month? John can be frustrated at that time element.

John has a proposal: *I want to go to soccer practice.*

That is clear. He finds happiness in going to soccer practice.

Then the father is negotiating. *Yes, you can go to soccer practice, but can you go next week?*

The dad is becoming clearer. He is accepting that John can go to practice but at a more appropriate time. But John is inflexible. He does not want to budge and compromise. Here, he is having difficulty taking the perspective of the other, thinking of possibilities and shifting his attention from his concern to another's.

But the father has also hit a wall. When he says, "you're grounded," he is effectively shutting out John and forcing him to do his will. As we have said, rewards and punishments are effective means of influencing the behavior of children. But it also reduces their capacity to decide logically about making the best decisions. You are punishing a kid for not following you. That is an approach that is appealing more to your power dynamics than to sound reasoning. If the child can learn to understand that it is better to follow your command because there is a greater value, the safety of your other child for example, to be gained, then they will see the logic better. Following the command becomes more acceptable because it is grounded on reasoning than merely an imposition of your power as a parent. When John hears "you're grounded," he simply does not want to come to the table at all. He abandons any pretense of a conversation and shuts the father out.

The key in this part is to allow the child to generate possibilities and alternatives that can be acceptable to both of you. When there is singular thinking, inflexibility is reinforced and the child does not mature. The working memory is important to develop. This allows the child to think of other ways of getting at the same target in a different way, one that can benefit others also. You can help your child generate these possibilities by inviting them to think. You can pose questions like "Can you think of another solution?" or "Do you see any other way, a different way to solve both of our problems?" They will really resist this first because they already have one solution: getting what they want. But when you continually ask them the question of alternatives, the mind will become more creative in generating possibilities. This is a skill you have to constantly develop in your children.

A loophole could be to understand the situation temporally. Let the child know that there is an appropriate time for everything. They want to have a toy or attend an event right now, but the circumstances are not optimal. You can ask them to think of postponing such demands until a more appropriate time. How about next week? Or next month? They will still get what they want, but they are able to delay gratification for the sake of a better good right now.

But be fair with the child also. You have to make an effort to consider your child's concerns and adjust your priorities to meet their demands. John has a point. His father is busy and does not have time to take care of them or to allow them to have a social life. John wants to appeal about his need for friends, and yet his father makes him feel guilty about setting that aside so that his father can work. For a real table conversation to work, both parties must exert an effort to think of possibilities at some cost to their personal agenda. In this case, the father can compromise by taking care of the daughter during weekends and allowing John to be with his friends. There is a sense of fairness because both parties sacrificed something so they can both benefit from the arrangement. If the father does not consider John's concern, then he is applying the *Me Perspective* and ends the conversation effectively. When you have more options to choose from, then you are able to make a better decision as a family.

Decide

From all these possibilities, you have to decide which option is best for all. It will matter to the child if the process you underwent was fair or not. If they feel that you just pushed them to do what you want, then the following becomes reluctant and you may face resistance. On your end, you also don't just want to give in for the sake of giving in. You need to know that your child understands the consequences and can appreciate the value of looking at possibilities.

There will be a lot of times when no definitive decision is made. The child will get tired of the exercise and you might also reach your limit of understanding. It happens. But there is no real pressure to decide immediately. Some decisions may take a long time before people realize the value of what was said during the conversation. Maybe, after talking to you, the child will realize that you have a point. He may not understand it during the table encounter because he is still too full of emotions. But when the feelings have subsided, they will have time to think. Respect that time and don't push them too hard to realize your point immediately.

You also have to think of yourself. Maybe you really need to listen to your child more, not just to what is being said. Understand the feeling that underlies your child's behavior. Is he seeking your attention? Are you there when he needs you? Does he long for something that he cannot tell you in concrete words? There is a struggle for each child to communicate their love to their parents. They love you more than you can imagine. Hence, be patient that these conversations will become fruitful in the future.

Make sure that the decision you both make is owned by the child. It is good if the decision is actually formulated by the child in his own words. There should be a sense of ownership when the course of action taken is freely chosen by the child. Otherwise, you dictated to him what to do and this will lead to problems with actually carrying out the decision. Invite the child to own the decision, not make it for him.

Of course, there are times when you need an answer immediately. It's ok to make those decisions, especially if safety is involved. But know that you can always revisit that situation with your child. You can plot all the available possibilities in a calmer environment should you be in that situation again. Don't feel as if every situation needs to have a solution immediately. Always involve your child and respect that they have good opinions too.

Chapter 7

Putting It All Together

· ♥ · ♥ · ♥ · ♥ · ♥ ·

At this point, you may have been bombarded with so much information on perspectives, approaches, skills, and other methods of creating effective communication with your child. I know it's too much, but you must have a sense of how to bring it all together. It will be difficult at first, especially if your child is resistant or if you panic quickly. The tendency is to stick with what we know, that is, to insist on our perspective or give in to the child. But we need to exert the effort to give this method a chance. Let's try out what you have learned by analyzing the following exchange.

"Mom, can I go to Nathan's house right now?" Robby said.

"Why honey? It's the middle of the night. You can go play with Nathan tomorrow morning." I reasoned out.

"But I have to go. Nathan and I are building this big Lego castle and we need to start it now." Robby was quite focused.

"Honey, it's 8 PM. Nathan is probably asleep right now. You should be asleep too. I will take you tomorrow."

"No Mom. We have to go now. I don't understand why you can't see how important this is to me." Robby was starting to whine.

"No, honey. It's just a Lego castle, it's not the end of the world. You can go tomorrow and that's final." I was starting to get exasperated.

"If you don't let me go to Nathan's, I will run away now." Robby fought back.

"Robby, don't test me tonight. I'm not in the mood. Just go to your room. Now!" I threatened.

"You're always like that. I hate you," Robby said bitterly.

"Just go to your room honey. We'll talk in the morning." I was quite taken aback.

Robby slams the door, stomps off and begins throwing things in his room.

What do you think about this exchange? Do you think it was handled well? Is there a better way to have approached the problem? This is the part where we apply everything we have learned so far about managing explosions.

First, we have to identify the problem. What is it that your child is having difficulty with? What are his triggers? List them down. Is it an executive skill problem, a language, emotional, or social skill problem? Defining the main problem is the first step in helping your kid. If you can pinpoint what exactly they need, then you can make the necessary intervention.

In this case, Robby seems to have a problem with his executive and emotional skills. He is so determined to go to his friend's house even in the middle of the night. When his mother tries to bargain with him, promising to take him the following morning, Robby still wouldn't budge. This shows a problem with working memory because he cannot think of the possibility of going at a more appropriate time. He has difficulty with interference because the thought of being needed by Nathan kept on recurring in his mind so much that he can't push it aside. And he has a problem with cognitive flexibility because he cannot imagine the possibility that Nathan might be asleep or that his mother is tired. He cannot put himself in the perspective of the other.

When he stomps off and throws stuff in his room, we see that Robby also has difficulty in managing his emotions. We should recognize the effort to go to his room because perhaps this calms him down. But there are safety warning signs that he can be quite destructive, as evidenced by throwing objects in his room. The anger is not proportional to his problem, and the way he expresses his anger is also a sign of deficiency.

Knowing that Robby has difficulties performing executive and emotional skills, you should target these in the next conversations. Don't miss the opportunity to teach them how to think of alternatives, imagine others' perspectives, and manage their emotions. Train them as soon as you recognize these difficulties.

Next is preparing for the table. You have to ask yourself what is your disposition in entering a conversation and what is it that you are exactly proposing. Ask yourself, "What am I feeling as I talk with my child? And am I very irritated? Do I feel an overwhelming sense of urgency?" You can postpone a conversation when you feel that you are not ready or that your feelings will cloud your openness. Also, be clear about what exactly you want to offer. "Is it doable? Is it reasonable? Can it be postponed?

Can the plan be changed?" It pays to be prepared when you go to the conversation. Just make sure that you are open to having your plan changed.

In the previous conversation, it is important to note what the condition of the mother was. She sounds welcoming at first. But as Robby continues to badger her, she becomes exasperated. This is normal because it is really difficult to hold lengthy conversations with explosive kids. She reaches a boiling point also and simply postpones the conversation in the morning. I actually feel that this is a good move on her part because she recognizes that she is not in an optimal mood to process Robby's feelings. She should just make sure that she follows up the next morning or when she and Robby are both ready. However, do not make it a habit to brush your child's concern because you just feel tired. We all do feel tired. So make the time out for your child and they will appreciate the effort.

Next, know all the proper timing of the conversation. Is the child in the normal stage? Is he already erupting? What approach would be best at this stage? Don't panic that an explosion is coming your way. If it happens, it happens. Just try to remain calm and think of the best time you can teach your child.

In the conversation, we see that the child transitioned quickly from the pre-explosion, explosion and post-explosion phases real quick. This is a child who gets triggered and explodes quickly. What is alarming in his actions is that he expresses his anger in a violent manner. But we also recognize his effort to go to his room and explode there. He is showing signs that he knows himself well. He knows he can hurt people and so he simply expresses himself in the safety of his room. This is a good coping mechanism for Robby.

And finally, try to follow the format that I prescribed. Remember the MIRROR-PROPOSE-DECIDE steps. The sequence is important because you cannot teach your kid to think about alternatives without first addressing their pressing emotions. From recognizing their emotions, lead them to also try understanding yours. State your clear propositions next. Make sure that they are doable and time-bound, with clear expectations. Explore other possibilities. Discuss what will work for you and what will work for your child. And then make a decision, however tentative it may be. Let your child own the decision, do not make it for them all the time.

Let's see how the mother could have addressed her son's concerns. But first, let's analyze how the conversation went.

Mom: Honey, it's 8 PM. Nathan is probably asleep right now. You should be asleep too. I will take you tomorrow.

Robby: No Mom. We have to go now. I don't understand why you can't see how important this is to me.

Mom: No, honey. It's just a Lego castle, it's not the end of the world. You can go tomorrow and that's final.

When we look at the mother's reply to Robby's assertion that she doesn't understand, we can see that the mother is dismissing Robby's giving importance to his castle-building with Nathan. Robby says he can't understand her. And the mother simply says Robby is overreacting. This type of reply of the mother invalidates what is important for Robby. Yes, maybe it is just a Lego castle, something very trivial for adults. But for Robby, it really means something. Maybe it's not just the Lego castle, but that fact that he is doing something with a friend, a connection he may not feel at home. So the mother could have easily picked that up as an invitation to inquire on how important Nathan is to her son.

Robby: If you don't let me go to Nathan's, I will run away now.

Mom: Robby, don't test me tonight. I'm not in the mood. Just go to your room. Now!

Robby: You're always like that. I hate you.

Mom: Just go to your room honey. We'll talk in the morning.

In this next part, there was an exchange of feelings but there was no invitation to empathize. The mother simply said she wasn't in the mood. Maybe she was tired from work, stressed with events outside the home, or simply distracted. But she didn't invite Robby to feel for her. Robby in turned expressed a very profound emotion, "I hate you." It's such a strong word for a child to say. You can get angry at your mother, irritated at times or annoyed. But hate really means something else, something deep and far-reaching. Hate can be a product of a prolonged sense of neglect or a chronic woundedness that the child is unable to process. The mother needs to investigate where her child is coming from when he uses the word 'hate' to describe his feelings for her.

I would recommend the following conversation to the mother to hopefully address the situation in a time they are both ready.

Mom: Hey honey, can we talk?

Robby: No Mom. I don't want to talk to you.

Mom: You don't want to talk to me. Can you tell me why?

Robby: Because I hate you.

Mom: You hate me. Why do you hate me?

Robby: Because you don't have time for me. You're always out of the house. And when you're here at home, you always don't allow me to go out with my friends.

Mom: Oh. I am sorry for that honey. I'm sorry I can't be with you all the time. But I am not always out of the house honey. Remember that I have work during the day, and I am here in the evening. I'm here during weekends. I'm sorry that I don't allow you to go to your friends. It's just that I worry about you and I miss you being here.

Robby: Oh. I didn't know that.

In this exchange, we see that Robby was able to vent out his feelings for his mother. In return, the mother said she was sorry if Robby had those feelings. Even if she wasn't at fault, the simple saying of "I'm sorry" already eases the hurt Robby feels. She also corrects Robby's use of 'always.' We should be very wary about hasty generalizations because they can really lead to incorrect thinking. When we say 'always,' the act is done on a daily basis. We should be more careful in making these generalizations because it may not be really the case. And lastly, the mother was able to share her own feelings of longing for Robby. There is a genuine desire to be with her child that causes her to be strict at times. This opening helps both parties to see where each other is coming from.

Mom: Ok, so what do you want to happen?

Robby: I want to go to Nathan's house right now and build the Lego castle with him.

Mom: Ok. Do you think Nathan is awake right now? Do you think he is in the mood to play with you? Maybe he is also tired.

Robby: Maybe, I don't know.

Mom: How about I take you in the morning? By that time, Nathan will be awake too and more ready to play with you.

Robby: But what about the Lego castle?

Mom: What do you think honey? Do you think you can still finish building it tomorrow?

Robby: I guess so.

Here we see that there is an invitation for Robby to think of alternatives. He is invited by his mother to think of Nathan's position, to see Robby's request from the perspective of Nathan. She is also asking Robby about the possibility of doing it at another time. Because of this, Robby is challenged to think of possibilities. When you explain these possibilities and the child is able to grasp them, then you have achieved some sort of progress. From considering the option, they might eventually choose that option.

Towards the end of your discussion, let the child choose at the end. Let the course of action you will take come from their words. In this way, there is a sense of ownership of the decision which will lead to a better following.

Mom: Ok so Robby, what is our decision?

Robby: I still want to go to Nathan's house.

Mom: But Nathan is probably asleep. I also want you to be rested so you could build the castle better tomorrow.

Robby: Alright then.

Mom: So what have you decided?

Robby: Yeah, I guess I will just go tomorrow. But it has to be tomorrow alright?

Mom: Sure, no problem honey. Go to sleep already. See you tomorrow.

Here we see that the mother is already assured of the decision. But she wants it to come from Robby. She doesn't want to say the decision out loud but wants Robby to say it. This is a good exercise in empowering the child to make good decisions. If you don't agree with the decision, then you can agree to disagree for the moment. You can make a temporary one and then resume the conversation when you are able to both feel good about the course of action. Remember that you don't always have to be right. You just have to follow the process of consulting and negotiating. In this way, you are teaching their minds to develop more than just resolving problems.

I know this exercise is ideal but might not work most of the time. Especially when you are in an explosion, kids can be very stubborn about their decisions. No matter how convincing you are, you might still end up giving in to your child or forcing your way through. Don't beat yourself up. This is a long process we are talking about, not an overnight transformation. Trust in the process and you will see the developments after months of practice. It will be really tiresome, but the fruits of this tedious process are very rewarding. It is ok to make mistakes but make sure that you exert effort to correct this the next time around. You don't want to end up with a teenager or an adult who are already set in their ways and are very difficult to reason out with.

Conclusion

· ❤ · ❤ · ❤ · ❤ · ❤ ·

Thomas still tests me at times. In spite of our conversations, there are times when Thomas just bursts. If he wants something, he will really make you know he wants it bad. There are times when he simply crumples on the ground when he doesn't get what he wants. It is at these moments that I feel I still need to teach him. I have trusted this method over the years and I feel that somehow, Thomas has become better at managing his emotions and controlling his impulses. I feel giddy when he is able to tell me, "Mom, I think I change my mind" or "Yeah, I see that now." These words tell me that somewhere in his brain, a new part is forming, a more mature and integrated part that will make Thomas easier to deal with and more prepared to take on new challenges.

I worry about him a lot. In our house, he has a protective space where he can be understood and respected. His antics don't go unpunished, in the sense that he will still have to suffer the consequences of breaking the rules. But he is able to be himself, fully expressive and active. I worry that outside of the house, he might not meet such understanding people. In school, he is quite shy with other kids. I worry that he might explode on one of them or on the teachers. So far, he has been able to manage his emotions. But as he grows up, I know that there will be a lot more people different than us. Our style of conversing with him, the invitation to think of possibilities, the challenge to emphasize, the consultative atmosphere, might not be shared by other people who just want to do things their way. I really hope that Thomas applies what he learns in our house to the outside world. I cannot talk to every teacher, coworker, partner, crush, salesperson, acquaintance and friend he might have in the future and explain to them Thomas' condition and how he should be approached. That would be smothering him and belittling his capacity to stand up for himself. But as parents, we can only do what we can now and hope that our efforts will pay off. I believe that Thomas and all the other explosive children in the world just want to be heard and loved like any other kid. Teach them, love them and they will love you back. The energy inside of them is just bursting to be channeled into something productive. Help them help themselves.

Leaving a Review

As a self-published author, I find it important not only to write great books but also provide my readers with the best value possible. Being an Indie writer means I don't have access to all the perks of a traditional publisher, such as a publicist to get the word out about my latest releases. That's where you come in. A little bit of your time can go a long way towards helping me spread the word and I would be most appreciative if you would consider posting your honest thoughts about this book on Amazon.

Your review remains one of the most valuable promotional tools available. Reviews are vital in helping new readers find books they will enjoy reading. So if you've enjoyed this book, please consider leaving an honest rating or review by going to this book's page on Amazon. Good ratings and reviews from readers can help me attract new readers who will also enjoy my writing.

Thank you for your support,

Grace

About the Author

· ❤ · ❤ · ❤ · ❤ · ❤ ·

Grace is a well-known parenting author who has written several books on the topic. She has dedicated her life to assisting families through her writings. Her greatest enjoyment in life is being a mother because it's the most gratifying job she's ever had. She likes to write books that touch on all the different aspects of parenting and personal experiences, such as her encounters with her children.

Her love for writing began when she discovered a parenting technique for her explosive son, who was diagnosed with ADHD and ODD, that outperformed others. She was determined to get the word out to other parents as soon as possible. With time, this has developed into something bigger where she is able to share great pieces of advice that can truly change lives.

She also incorporates insights from other parents to offer an enlightening reading experience for all of her readers. Grace hopes that families will be inspired to change the way they think and make better parenting decisions by reading her books.

She enjoys reading novels and watching movies with her family on the weekends.

Visit her profile on Amazon to learn more about her other works - **https://www.amazon.com/author/gracecohen**

Printed in Great Britain
by Amazon